DiRTY STOP OUTS GUIDE TO 1970s Birmingham

By Jim and Ron Simpson

Prime Minister
Edward Heath at
the Mulberry Bush
pub after the IRA
bombings

Starring:

Rum Runner	Mothers	Barbarella's
Tow Rope	The Crown	Locarno
Opposite Lock	The Barrel Organ	Rebecca's and more

Jim and Ron Simpson assert the moral right to be identified as the authors of this work.
A catalogue record for this book is available from the British Library.

Published by Dirty Stop Outs Ltd.

Other titles in this series:

Dirty Stop Out's Guide to 1970s Manchester.

Dirty Stop Out's Guide to 1970s Liverpool.

Dirty Stop Out's Guide to 1970s Coventry.

Dirty Stop Out's Guide to 1970s Barnsley.

Dirty Stop Out's Guide to 1950s Sheffield.

Dirty Stop Out's Guide to 1960s Sheffield.

Dirty Stop Out's Guide to 1970s Sheffield.

Dirty Stop Out's Guide to 1980s Sheffield.

Dirty Stop Out's Guide to 1980s Sheffield – King Mojo Edition

Dirty Stop Out's Guide to 1990s Sheffield.

Dirty Stop Out's Guide to 1970s Chesterfield.

Dirty Stop Out's Guide to 1970s Sheffield – Club Fiesta Edition.

Dirty Stop Out's Guide to 1980s Chesterfield.

Dirty Stop Out's Guide to 1980s Coventry.

Dirty Stop Out's Guide to Coventry's Working Mens' Clubs

Dirty Stop Out's Guide to 1980s Sheffield – The Limit Edition

Dirty Stop Out's Guide to 1980s Chesterfield Quizbook.

Dirty Stop Out's Guide to 1990s Chesterfield.

Dirty Stop Out's Guide to 1980s Sheffield – Wapentake Edition.

Dirty Stop Outs Guide to 1980s Chesterfield – In Pictures.

Dirty Stop Outs Guide to Sheffield – Rebels Edition.

We're on the look out for writers to cover other UK towns and cities and we're always on the look out for great retro photos! Please email us at **info@dirtystopouts.com** if you fancy getting involved.

DiRTY STOP OUTS GUIDE TO 1970s Birmingham

By Jim and Ron Simpson

Rum Runner
Tow Rope
Opposite Lock

Mothers
The Crown
The Barrel Organ

Barbarella's
Locarno
Rebecca's and more

Football violence was commonplace in the era

Contents

| DECEMBER | No. 1 | NO CHARGE |

SEX CHANGE SNAKE IN DRUG PROBE SCANDAL

Nigel Phillips

Editorial

"Big Bear," a monthly gazette of

Reptile rape on runway

RETURNING from Germany last week, Tea and Symphony's 24th brightly coloured cloth snake, Herbert, was subjected to a rigorous customs search from Heathrow officials. The Birmingham-based snake was cleared only after exhaustive personal and baggage checks.

The snake had been returning from Bremen with the group, where they had been appearing on the huge Eurovision show, "Beat Club," which goes out to over 34 million viewers throughout the world.

Group members, James Langston, Jef Daw and Nigel Phillips were quickly cleared as customs as usual, but Herbert was extremely

was unable to comment on the situation.

The following day Tea and Sym-phony travelled to

James Langston

Jeff Daw

Above: The first edition of *Big Bear* magazine, the scandal that never was

Right: Readers' response in *Big Bear* 2

LETTERS TO BIG BEAR

DEAR BIG BEAR, — Being highly suspicious, by nature, of the high-pressure, hyping balderdash that music biz moguls pile on desk with unerring diligence, I was surprised to find that "Big Bear" was refreshing, unpretentious and honest, whilst still managing to do a valid job, communicating information for basically commercial reasons. I firmly believe that there need not be such a significant dichotomy between business and creativity, and "Big Bear" number one is a step in the direction of proving this.

Furthermore, although I labour the point to the verge of becoming utterly boring, it's about time that the progressive music business (and the Underground in general) decentralised itself, and Birmingham, as our second city, ought therefore to respond to its often excellent musicians and do something about it.

Best wishes, and that'll be ten quid you owe me! Good-night.
MARK WILLIAMS
'International Times'
Alias Spark.

☆ ☆ ☆

DEAR BIG BEAR, — Thanks for your paper. It's very nice, and if it's a personal at-

tempt to publicise local bands, it's extra nice. How is it free? Learnt lots from it—e.g., I didn't know Mike Kellie and Polly Palmer were ex-Locomotive.

Can you keep sending them? Too much.
PETE,
Editor, 'Zigzag'

☆ ☆ ☆

DEAR BIG BEAR, — Many thanks for your first issue, which I read with interest. I am not a Birmingham man myself, but I have always been under the impression that Brum is rather a wasteland, apart from one or two notable clubs. I imagine that the bands featured in the paper are all Birmingham-based, and this has given me great hope for the emergence of the city as a musical centre in its own right—perhaps as Britain's Motown.

As your city is the second largest in the country, I feel that it should have something to offer on the musical scene. If the standard of your first issue is maintained, "Big Bear" should be among the strong voices in the musical paper world.

Love and peace.
JOHN HOGG.
Essex University.

DEAR SIR,—Having obtained a copy of 'Big Bear' through 'Zigzag,' and having found it an absolute gas, I am now writing to you to try and obtain this paper each month.

Love and peace.

STEVE.
Elgin, Morayshire.

☆ ☆ ☆

Whilst the 'Birmingham Post' said :—

"More evidence of the progress and sophistication of the Birmingham pop scene came recently in the form of a publication called 'Big Bear.' It is produced by Big Bear of Edgbaston and contains news stories and information about groups Tea & Symphony, Locomotive, Black Sabbath and Sacrifice. So well produced is 'Big Bear' that it took some time to realise that this was a new underground newspaper.

"Yes, it's fair to say that the Birmingham pop scene has come of age."

COLLIN MALHAM
Pop Music Critic.

Foreword

The headline screamed, "Sex Change Snake in Drug Probe Scandal" which leaves little to the imagination. The publication was named *Big Bear*, the era was the dawn of the 1970s and the reason for the publication's existence was not complicated. It was born out of my frustration at the consistent lack of interest in the great music coming out of Birmingham, the UK Capital of Rock and Roll.

That headline? It came out of a conversation with a veteran journalist when I mentioned my intention to launch *Big Bear*. He told me not to underestimate the importance of an attention-grabbing headline for the first edition. He told me it was commonly accepted in the newspaper biz that such headlines should include references to drugs and sex, that a mention of reptiles never went amiss and the word "scandal" was essential. I responded accordingly.

So that was how the 1970s music scene started for me, increasingly angry that the bands I managed were touring,

> **...such headlines should include references to drugs and sex, that a mention of reptiles never went amiss and the word "scandal" was essential.**

attracting enthusiastic audiences and building visibly, had record deals with majors, but seemed unable to get gigs in the London area or to attract any interest from the London-based media. The bands in question were The Locomotive, Bakerloo, Tea & Symphony and Black Sabbath.

As it happened, *Big Bear* only ran for three monthly editions before the demands of managing the sudden charting of the Black Sabbath album took all my attention. Interestingly, this seemingly overnight success came despite consistently demeaning reviews: "The music made by this trio (trio?) is the sort you think you have heard a million times before.

A very hairy Jim Simpson with blues great Muddy Waters

The idea was simple, putting it into practice far more challenging, complicated, fascinating, exciting and satisfying than I could ever have imagined.

Sadly unoriginal," opined *Sounds*. The *Melody Maker* dispensed sarcastic advice: not to let children under 16 buy the album, not to let those of a nervous disposition listen alone, not to listen at all if you wanted to hear something new. Very helpful!

With Sabbath suddenly touring internationally, television, radio, concerts, festivals and record deals negotiated in Europe, Japan and the USA, my hands were full. There was no time for the Big Bear publication; sex change snakes would have to wait.

The week that *Paranoid* topped both the single and album charts was the week that Black Sabbath walked away. Litigation followed, of course, and we had a pyrrhic victory in the High Courts with a modest award that took some 14 years to get paid in full. It was a time for self-evaluation. I decided that there was no point in discovering new talent and building a career to the point where the sharp suits decide it's worthwhile to come in with felonious intent, leaving me to start all over again.

So, with the 1970s barely two years old, I changed tack and went back to an earlier passion, American blues – and it was to make my presence on the Birmingham scene more fragmentary for a few years.

The idea was simple, putting it into practice far more challenging, complicated, fascinating, exciting and satisfying than I could ever have imagined. The European blues boom in the 1960s had propelled a handful of blues artists to enduring fame – B. B. King, Muddy Waters, John Lee Hooker, Freddie King and the like – but that left scores of great bluesmen scuffling, playing on street corners for tips and taking on badly paid menial jobs to scrape a living. We found Lightnin' Slim stoking furnaces in a Pontiac foundry, Doctor Ross sweeping floors at General Motors, Whispering Smith building swimming pools in Louisiana, Washboard Willie driving a school bus in Detroit. And so it went on.

From 1972 to the end of the decade Birmingham became the base for UK and European tours for some 32 American bluesmen and most of them recorded for Big Bear.

But, if I was taken off the Birmingham scene for tours, sometimes of 40-odd days, the Birmingham scene wasn't about to leave me alone. So far as Big Bear Records were concerned, I certainly wasn't looking beyond my work with American bluesmen, but, if you accidentally stumble across a talent, it's hard to turn your back. I believed – and still do – that Muscles from California (that's the Birmingham suburb) were the best of the blue-eyed soul bands. We recorded them for an album and a bunch of singles for *Big Bear* and they toured the UK in support of The Ohio Players, The Fatback Band, Earth, Wind and Fire, and more.

Then there was Garbo (not his real name) who wrote stunning songs which he recorded for Big Bear and was carving out a promising career – until he discovered punk. Admittedly he wrote great punk songs, sang fiercely and played stunning guitar, but it was just too big a leap from lush ballads to his *Only Death is Fatal Big Bear* single with Garbo's Celluloid Heroes.

One morning in 1978 I came to work to find a cassette pushed through the letterbox. I played it with my morning coffee, picked myself up from the floor and contacted Josh Jones, leader of The Quads, who told me the cassette had picked up eight straight rejections from record companies.

I visited Zella Recording Studios and over-dubbed some wildly enthusiastic applause, and The Quads had a Number 66 hit with *There Must be Thousands*.

That was in 1979 and a nice way to see out the decade. Coincidentally the seventies ended as they began, with my plans for another Birmingham-based monthly music paper coming to fruition. It was called *Brum Beat*, it was there to celebrate the great bands of our city and the headline of the first edition bore no references to drugs, sex or even reptiles, but was rather more to the point: "Brum Beat Hits the Road".

Jim Simpson

Introduction:
A city on the move

New Street in the 1970s

I n 1965 Roy Smith, a reporter on the *Birmingham Evening Mail*, described a new road interchange, then in the planning stage, as "a cross between a plate of spaghetti and an unsuccessful attempt at a Staffordshire knot." When the Gravelly Hill Interchange opened in 1972, it was already permanently identified as Spaghetti Junction. The junction, linking the nation's motorway network with the A38(M) thrusting right into a city centre pitching itself towards a bright shiny future, somehow summed up Birmingham in the seventies as a city going places.

When the new Birmingham Repertory Theatre, opened in 1971, wanted to celebrate the city in a revue, what better name than *Up Spaghetti Junction*? Birmingham was a city on the move and through the 1970s, despite unrest and tragedy, Birmingham lived up to its motto, FORWARD, especially when moving forward took you to a pub or club.

Unrest and tragedy there certainly were. In the UK generally the 1970s were a time when ordinary lives were constantly disrupted by the effects of industrial unrest and

> **In the UK generally the 1970s were a time when ordinary lives were constantly disrupted by the effects of industrial unrest and the IRA's terror campaign**

the IRA's terror campaign – and Birmingham was at the centre of both. One of the first skirmishes in the conflict that led to Edward Heath's Three Day Week and James Callaghan's Winter of Discontent was at Saltley Coking Plant in 1972. The Battle of Saltley Gate, with miners' flying pickets taking on the massed ranks of police, prevented fuel supplies from leaving the depot – and incidentally saw the emergence of one Arthur Scargill. Possibly the other most controversial union leader of the time, Derek Robinson ("Red Robbo"), equally divisive and equally vilified by the right-wing press, was Birmingham-based at British Leyland in Longbridge where the 1970s were certainly not a time of peace.

The Bull Ring and Rotunda

FIFTEEN MILLION POUNDS FOR THIS?

THE ESCALATING PROBLEMS OF THE NEW LIBRARY

Unless drastic and politically embarrassing steps are taken within the next few years, Birmingham's new Central and Reference Library will become an expensive and disastrous flop. It is now apparent that in a building designed to last a century the Reference Library is acutely short of space. The Social Sciences Department cannot house its present stock let alone its future acquisitions. Even the Philosophy and Religion Department – hardly an intellectual boom area – will be full in an estimated ten years. A converted chapel in Loscella, the mainstay of the old library, and due for closure on completion of the new one, is still used as a store house. It is in fact the only major source of expansion available to the Library.

'to last a century ….'

In September this year a Library spokesman told the 'Evening Mail' "It is true the Library was built to last a hundred years. But no one would pretend the estimate included provision for storage to last a century". The same day's 'Birmingham Post' in an article headed 'Storage problem looms for new Library', reported Cllr Ken Barton, Chairman of the City Leisure Services Committee as saying that he was not aware of the problem. Only a few days later he'd recovered from his suprise to tell the 'Mail': "It's been a long time, but now Birmingham and the surrounding areas have the finest Library complex in Europe."

It has indeed been a long time. It is now thirty-five years since the City approved construction of a new library to replace the one built in 1882. The present building is the brainchild of the John Madin Design Group, in association with the City Architect (who is suspended and faces conspiracy charges), and with the close co-operation of the City Librarian, W A Taylor. The result of this trio's operations is a pretentious structure of little merit as a public building and dismally un-

suited to its purpose. Much of the Library's publicity devolved around its so-called 'flexibility', but a building hung in the air cannot readily create more space for itself. Unlike the Library at Birmingham University, which over the past few years has doubled its size by adding new wings, the Reference Library is stuck with what it has got. Stuck presumably for the next 100 years.

Existing space can be more economically used by eventually replacing the present reserve stacks with a mobile, electronically operated stack system. But this scheme has drawbacks. It will increase the time taken to locate books for readers, and will be prone to technical failures. Service to the public will almost inevitably deteriorate. The only sensible solution to the problem, and one which has been diligently avoided, at least in public, is to have an annex built as near as possible to the main library, and as soon as possible. Acceptance of this idea would, however, be tantamount to admitting that Europe's largest custom-built public library is a failure.

The library has long been a thorn in Birmingham's flesh, becoming widely unpopular almost as soon as it began to take shape. Nor did the attitude of the architect help matters. In 1971 a Madin spokesman told the Sunday Mercury that it was designed to be simple but should have "expensive ornaments". "If the city cannot afford these things," he added, "then perhaps industry should donate them".

'mounting costs'

The steadily mounting costs of the building, which should have been completed in 1971, are a further cause of concern. The original 1967 estimate was £3½ million. A whole storey was lopped off to save money – a direct cause of the present space problem – but the saving was soon lost and for at least the last two years the local press has been referring ad

nauseam to the "new £3½ million Central Library", even when the evidence of its own columns indicates that this figure is badly in need of revision. In January this year the 'Post' reported that: "When the final bill...is paid later this year it is likely to be considerably higher than the original £3½ million".

In June, Alderman Beaumont Dark put the cost at "Well over £4 million". A month later the 'Mail' reported the demand of the General Purposes Committee for an investigation into the hold-up and rising costs. Emphasis on building costs moreover hides the full cost to the city; interest charge and repayments on the borrowed capital could well be in excess of £15 million.

'leaking roof'

Space and finance are not the Library's only problems. Penny pinching in the building and fitting out of the Library has brought many problems. The roof leaks, as do several of the inadequate toilets. The plumbing has been given an (unofficial) estimated life span of six years. An electrician has condemned the wiring system a potentially highly dangerous. The escalators have already undergone a major overhaul and the impractical continuous strips of bright orange carpeting are showing wear after only a few months.

It is depressing to conclude that as a result of self indulgent, short sighted planning, an expensive and prestigious public amenity can be kept viable in the lon term only by spending more public money. Following the same costly pattern as Cannon Hill Art Centre and with the Museum and Art Gallery claiming a desperate need for new premises, the fiasco of the Reference Library can only give ammunition to philistines of whatever persuasion, and lay a blight on any possibility of a bold approach to the enlivenment of Birmingham's cultural environment in the future.

Richard Wray.

Worse than power cuts and a reduced working week was the constant fear of IRA attacks. So often were schools or offices evacuated after mysterious phone calls that the term "bomb hoax" became as familiar as "traffic jam" as an explanation or excuse, but too often the attacks were real – and Birmingham experienced one of the worst, the deadliest act of terror in England between the Second World War and the 2005 London bombings. Just before 8.30 on the evening of November 21st, 1974, bombs exploded in the Mulberry Bush pub in one of the new Birmingham's iconic buildings, the Rotunda, and the Tavern in the Town in New Street. A third bomb in a branch of Barclay's Bank did not explode. The aftermath of the pub bombings is murky, with the unsafe convictions of the Birmingham Six and such disputed matters as the warning that never was – was an out-of-action public phone the reason for the heavy loss of life? But the simple tragic statistic for the pub-goers of Birmingham was 21 dead and 182 injured, many of them with seriously life-changing injuries. A large proportion of the victims were young people, even teenagers.

So it's a pretty wonderful comment on Brummies' ability to enjoy themselves that the 1970s are remembered so joyously by so many. Take John Kennedy, for instance:

"I came to Brum in 1972 aged 18 to train as a teacher and get drunk on a juicy grant – it was OK back then. We used to drink in The Greyhound up Lee

Bank near Davenport's. We drank in the standard bar where there was no spit-and-sawdust on the floor. We drank Bo&O, i.e. Strongbow and Orange, although it certainly wasn't Strongbow there. It was 10p a pint. John, the gaffer, was a giant of a tyrant and a Blues fanatic. He jumped over the bar once because some lads came in wearing Villa scarfs. I swear on my honour we saw him pick up one of those round, three-legged cast iron tables – with his teeth! And, as for the toilets..."

Chris Pitt was a similar age:

Le Metro in Livery Street, a firm favourite of Christine Fox, was another with a well-remembered balcony, complete with spiral staircase

---

"Having reached the age of 17 in 1970 it was the decade when going to gigs vied only with my childhood love and obsession with horse-racing. At that age I felt part of town and town felt part of me. Spending Saturday nights at the Alhambra pub (yes, I know I was underage) or the Golden Eagle on Hill Street, reading the *Sports Argus* and waiting for the guy to arrive with his seafood snacks ('Cockles, mussels, whelks, prawns' was his signature cry), then getting a greasy hotdog or hamburger from the stand near Victoria Square before getting the last bus home."

Not all pubs had the rough-and-ready charms of The Greyhound. The Parisian in Needless Alley is recalled with affection by many – especially for its stylish gallery:

"It had a gallery where you could drink your pint and look down on the floor below." (Andrew Harris)

"It was fabulous. Overlooking the balcony with the DJ and the dance floor. I only ever went on a lunchtime during the work day. Best hour of the day." (Julia Rose)

"It wasn't Friday if we didn't have a few at Parisian and Le Pub." (Deb Wagleigh)

"A great place at weekends. Normally a fair-sized queue to get in – unless you knew the doorman." (Tony Powell)

Jim Cronin is certain that the big hit song when the Parisian opened was *In the Summertime* by Mungo Jerry – so that's 1970, then.

Le Metro in Livery Street, a firm favourite of Christine Fox, was another with a well-remembered balcony, complete with spiral staircase.

Chris Pitt is clearly the sort of chap who likes to be organised, even when having fun. He even rated every band he saw on a scale from A to E and kept meticulous diaries which throw up a varied mix of well-remembered favourite clubs and the odd totally forgotten surprise:

"The diaries revive the names of long-lost music venues such as the Mayfair Suite, Barbarella's and Henry's Blueshouse at the Crown. Birmingham and Aston Universities were also popular locations, along with (for a brief period) late night Friday sessions at the Brum Studio (at the Birmingham Rep

Lee Longlands- 1970s car park opening

Page 8   REDBRICK, September 29, 1978   Page 9

THIS IS BIRMINGHAM...

A GUIDE FOR YOUR SURVIVAL......

Compiled by Grace
Photos Roger Emmott

THE ROTUNDA

A round office block towering over the Bull Ring in the city centre. It has become an internationally known symbol of the city.

The Rotunda

BULL RING

Houses the indoor market, the same as above but also selling meat and fish and anything ranging from Goldfish and crocodiles to the latest LP's and any length of material you require.

OPEN MARKET

The ideal place to buy cheap fruit and veg. Also cheap articles of clothing though the quality cannot be guaranteed.

A scene on a busy Saturday morning at the Market.

SHOPPING CENTRE

Above this is the Railway Station and the shopping centre. Here you will find most of the things you require in the way of consumer goods and clothing. However the more famous names in shopping, C & A, Lewis's, Rackhams, Marks and Sparks, B.H.S. etc. are to be found in the main shopping streets. Corporation Street, New Street, Broad Street and the High Street.

EATING PLACES

Cheap and fairly edible; Cassidy's Wimpy Bars for Hamand Beefburgers. Great American Disaster is better, also good for pancakes and waffles. Pizzaland the USA version of Italian food is OK as long as you have not been spoilt by real Italian Pizzas. The Happy Gathering is the city centre chinese eatin place and well worth a visit when you don't have much money and are hungry. On the other hand if you have £5 to spare then the Danish Food Centre is the place for you.

DRINKING PLACES

are few and far between in the city centre unless you like very crowded bars or are looking for the live music entertainments (see music page). A section for Teddy's on New Street, the scene of the IRA bombings in 1974, but now totally renovated. Löwenbräu's Beer cellar sells real german beer. There are alternatives to pubs in the form of Winebars, of which there are at least 3 in the centre, Willies in Summer Row, a good one on the Queensway and Winston's in Cannon Street. To be avoided at all costs is Yates's Vine Lodge.

WHAT TO DO ON A RAINY DAY

A rainy day can well be spent either in the Art Gallery and Museum (opposite the Library) or the Science Museum in New Hall Street. Don't groan at the idea of museums and art galleries. They really are worth a visit. The art gallery houses the largest collection of pre-Raphaelite paintings in the country and at the Science Museum you can while away the hours pushing buttons and watching the lights flash on and off or see a full size steam locomotive called the City of Birmingham once along its track.

Queen Victoria outside the Civic Centre

THE LIBRARY

The library , a complex concrete monstrosity, is the largest in the country and has an excellent reference section and you can also borrow records from the very comprehensive record library. There are also ample facilities for private study in the reference section. Like most public buildings in Birmingham, it's built across a road.

The Library.

WMPTE

Transport in Brum

Birmingham is, on the whole, well served by public transport. Buses and trains are fairly heavily subsidised, and are considerably cheaper than in most other towns. It now costs 8½p to travel into town from the University, whether you choose to go by bus (61, 62 or 63 from Bristol Road to Navigation St) or by train (every fifteen minutes from the University Railway Station next to the medical school, to New Street Station. British Rail also do a cheap two-person day return costing 35p. The only condition is that both people travel together both ways. But it's a cheap way to get into town

and the train is certainly faster than the bus.

If you use Public Transport frequently it may be worthwhile getting a four-week travelcard for £8.50 + 50p registration for the first card. The travelcard is valid on any bus in the Birmingham area and on one train route.

The major complaint about W.M.P.T.E. is the night service. Although most areas are within reach of a night bus, the price is steep (40p flat fare). If there are more than two of you it is often worth getting a taxi which will deliver you to your own front door. There are night taxi ranks at New St. Station and in Stevenson Street (outside Birmingham Shopping Centre).

MAP LEGEND

1. Town Hall
2. ABC New Street Cinema
3. Arts Lab
4. Futurist Cinema
5. Gaumont Cinema
6. Odeon Queensway
7. Odeon New Street
8. Hippodrome
9. Repertory Theatre
10. Arts Shop
11. Public Library
12. Museum and Art Gallery
13. Science Museum
14. Barbarella's
15. Rebeccas

A. Bus Stop 61, 62, 63 to University
B. Bus Stop 3 to The Vale, 21 to Medical School
C. Bus Stop 62N to University Night Service.

BIRMINGHAM ARTS SHOP

If you are too lazy to book your theatre tickets at the actual Theatre, or if you are not quite sure what show you want to see, then the Arts Shop is the place for you. There you can book and pay for tickets for almost any Show in the West Midlands. You receive a coupon which is exchanged at the Theatre box-office on the night of your choice. The Arts Shop has a good selection of Posters at normal prices also greetings cards and good quality stationery.

CANALS

Away from the hustle-bustle of the shopping area in fact less than five minutes' walk away you can walk along the canal towpaths and sample the delights of 19th century Birmingham from the back. The towpath is a good place to go if you want to get away from it all. The canal is in the process of being renovated, the locks rebuilt and there's a good pub behind the Rep called the Longboat.

Within walking distance of the Vale are the Botanical Gardens. A horticultural paradise amidst the urban sprawl of edgbaston. A pleasant place to go for an evening stroll. During the summer, bands regularly give concerts on Sunday afternoons. There is also an aviary with a parrot house.

GRAPEVINE Page 12

Steve Rumbelow has said 'The actor, if trained properly, should be capable of great physical and mental feats .. The actor is like a sportsman, the harder he works the more pleased is the spectator' The actors' movements, particularly those of Hamlet were stylised, energetic, the posturing reminiscent of wrestlers. A naturalistic sequence of movements would be accepted without demanding the dramatic relevance of each part - but every motion of this posturing seemed to demand that its relevance be understood, yet often detracted from the speech to the extent of becoming totally alien. Merely as a general level of physical expression it was too forceful, as an expression parallel to the speech it was too complex.

The whole production was taken at a rapid pace which I felt would have proved confusing without an adequate background knowledge of the play. For me it was a personal assault, its distilled, particularly in the physical proximity of the person to person encounters, a mental brutality from the play- and I was left more confused than usual about the psychology of Hamlet's inability to act than in a traditional production.

s.m.d.

IN TOWN

ARTS LAB, Tower Street, Newtown, B19 3UY
Tel: 359 4192 Presents experimental and fringe groups.
THE FREEHOLD COMPANY in BEOWULF, the Anglo-saxon epic, Feb 8-10 inc. at 8.00pm.
STORYTELLER in late night shows on Feb 9th and 10th. 11pm. Storyteller are a group of actors from the Midlands Arts Theatre Company at Cannon Hill. Their individual musical talents, they play organ, guitars, sax and drums form the basis for their roadshow, which after appearances at the Lab and Cannon Hill they hope to tour in local Youth clubs. The theme is ' a suburban Adam and

a pre-packed Eve...... Follow Adam in his search for happiness to the Mate of the Year Contest.'

BIRMINGHAM REPERTORY THEATRE, Broad Street, B1 2EP
Box Office 236 4455 Mon-Sat 10am-8.00pm
(non-performance days to 6.00pm)
Students may buy any remaining ticket at 40p half an hour before the show. OAP's matinee tickets at 15p.
TREASURE ISLAND Daily evening performances til Feb 10th. also Wed and Sat matinees.
Feb12th-17th BALLET RAMBERT one week visiting season. Two programmes of works by contemporary choreographers. Mon-Wed eves TIS GOODLY SPORT, RICERCARE,4PIECES FOR 6 DANCERS, RAG DANCES, Thurs- Sat (&Sat mat.) CONSIDERING THE LILIES, TIC-TACK, LISTEN TO THE MUSIC, SIGOURAT.
From Feb 22nd for a month Rep & Studio companies in UP SPAGHETTI JUNCTION - or the Second City Show.
BRUM STUDIO at the Rep.
to Feb 3rd, and Feb 12th -17th Samuel Beckett's ENDGAME , his masterpiece of comic despair.
QUADS - a festival of visiting theatre groups Feb 26th-Mar 24th.
Feb 26,27th A LOVER OF DISTINCTION performed by EMMA the touring company of the East Midlands Arts Association.
BIRMINGHAM THEATRE (HIPPODROME) Hurst St., B5
Box Office 622 2576
to Feb 24th Pantomime - CINDERELLA with Dickie Henderson & Arthur Askey. Evenings daily and matinees Wed, Thur, Sat.
ALEXANDRA THEATRE Suffolk St. Ringway
Box Office 643 1231 10am to curtain rise.
PUSS IN BOOTS All month. Evenings Daily and matinees Mon, Wed, Thur, & Sat.
ASTON UNIVERSITY CENTRE FOR THE ARTS, Gosta Green
Tel 359 3611 Extns. 709 or 6287
N.F. Simpson's THE HOLE
WAITING FOR GODOT by Samuel Beckett.
For dates and times ring above.

---

when the theatre crowd had gone home) which largely focused on folk music where I saw Martin Carthy, Bridget St. John and even (bizarrely) Spike Milligan."

Cheryl Keysell and Julia Rose take up the story. Cheryl saw "ABC in the Holy City Zoo, Human League in Faces (of all places), Bronski Beat in Snobs, all random bands back in the day in clubs we all knew and loved," while Julia picks out "Joe Brown and his Bruvvers at Bingley Hall, Status Quo at the Plaza, Spencer Davis at the Elbow, Santana in St. Tropez and the Average White Band at the Odeon."

Andrew Harris summed it all up in a two-word phrase, "Bostin' days". His list of memorable music moments

---

Birmingham stop outs were trained up from an early age. Alison Clare Farngalo remembers Saturday mornings for Under 18s at the Locarno for those not old enough to drink:

---

stretches "from local greats like Ricky Cool and the Icebergs at the Barrel Organ, Digbeth, and Steve Gibbons at the Golden Eagle, Hill Street, to legends like John Cale (ex-Velvet Underground) at the Town Hall and Bob Marley and the Wailers at the Odeon, New Street."

John Kennedy, whom we last heard of braving the toilets at The Greyhound, found his way to some more salubrious places:

"I saw The Doors, sans Morrison, at The Mayfair in 1972, I think. The support band was Hawkwind who'd just had much of their gear stolen and the singer made some extremely un-hippy/New Age comments about it. In 1973 or '74 I saw the Steve Gibbons Band at their peak in the cellar at The Hippodrome – was it The Incognito? They had to stop mid-afternoon because the bingo had started."

Famous names, but what of the forgotten bands, many of them with those wonderfully bizarre names so popular at the time? And, for that matter, are they forgotten? That meticulous chronicler of 1970s Birmingham night-life, Chris Pitt, asks, clearly half-expecting a negative, "Anyone remember Angus, Fred Athens Wood, Mainline Dreamboat, Rock Rebellion or Walrus Gumboot?" Well, actually, Chris, quite a few people, certainly in the case of Walrus Gumboot. Tom Ward enthuses:

"Loved Walrus Gumboot – saw them many times. What was that song? *Thursday Morning?*"

Birmingham stop outs were trained up from an early age. Alison Clare Farngalo remembers Saturday mornings for under 18s at the Locarno for those not old enough to

drink: "Saturday morning disco, roller disco too – it was the place to hang out, meet others and have fun." And dance to Judge Dredd, according to Debbie Pickering.

Young Malcolm Hill served his apprenticeship in stopping out elsewhere:

"My first stop-out venues when I'd just left school at 15 were The Rainbow and The Mayfair dances. Prior to that it was the Silver Blades Ice Rink."

Bernadette Jarvis agrees: "I loved the Silver Blades on a Friday night. I think it was called The Heartbeat – great music on ice."

So there you! Hopefully this book will prove the accuracy of Alison Clare Farngalo's confident assertion:

"Growing up in seventies Brum was the best!"

sunshine

bullsheet

Once upon a time, in the town of Stratford lived a famous playwrite, 'William Shakespeare' was his name perhaps the most famous lines he ever wrote, appeared in his play 'Hamlet'.
Those lines were:-
'To be or not to be, that is the question'.
Upon those lines an established Birmingham Rock Group, now base their hopes and ideas. They are known as 'WALRUS GUMBOOT'. Four highly talented musicians, who have hit out at the dull Rock Scene in Birmingham, with there fast and exciting music. Already acclaimed by many, to be the most outstanding group in Birmingham on the semi-professional front.
Then why are they not a professional group, you may ask? Well, for a group such as 'WALRUS GUMBOOT', it is the same old story, lack of publicity, but for a group that is forward thinking and holds such high ideals about themselves and their music, very soon everything will change. For believe me friends they will be a name to be reckoned with.
The Personnell of the Group:-
JIM SLATER; Lead Guitar, A fast flowing guitarist, with an excellent showman streak in him.
TERRY LAWSON; Rythumn Guitar and Lead Vocalist.. Many have said that the days of the Rythumn Guitar are long gone, but Terry will tell you different.
DAVE MULLEN; Drums and Vocals. The main driving force behind th Group. Songwriter, Drummer, Showman and Vocalist, what more can one say.
PETE SLATER; Bass Guitar and Vocals. Establishing himself fast as a very 'Funky' and inventive Bass Guitarist.
After witnessing 'WALRUS GUMBOOT' live you will obviously agree with me,that the days of the lifeless heavy groups are certainly numbered. On August Bank Holiday, quite recently, 'WALRUS GUMBOOT', supported 'Stackridge' at Malvern Winter Gardens, Worcestershire. 'Stackridge' whose reputation, stretches far and wide were always, very good.The audience had obviously come to listen and enjoy their favourite group, but after 'WALRUS GUMBOOT' played their set, the crowd screamed for more. Such is the very electric atmosphere created by the group. The need in Birmingham now is for a group, with a different approach to pave the way on which others may follow. A new group to hold a guiding light as did Cream in the sixties. 'WALRUS GUMBOOT', might hold that light, the need for a group of this calidre is an obvious asset to any Rock Scene, but especially to Birmingham's.
For the future 'WALRUS GUMBOOT' are certainly 'to be'
See you around.

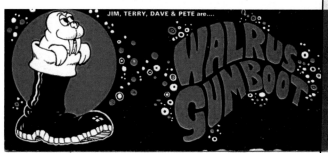

So this is Walrus Gumboot...

DiRTY STOP OUTS GUIDE

Alpha Tower – City Centre re-development

Prime Minister
Edward Heath at
the Mulberry Bush
pub after the IRA
bombings

22nd April 1976
Max Jones
Melody Maker
24/34 Meymott Street
London SE1 9LU

} *sent to home address to save time.*

Dear Max

Here is the up-to-date news from Big Bear.
COUSIN JOE FROM NEW ORLEANS currently touring Holland,
Belgium,France,Germany and Scandinavia,comes to Britain
in early May to play CANTERBURY Kent University(May 11)
BANGOR Arts Festival(12) BLACKPOOL Pleasure Beach Casino(13)
CRANFIELD Institute Of Technology(14) BRISTOL University(15)
NOTTINGHAM Trent Bridge Inn(16) ROTHERHAM Arts Centre(17)
NEWCASTLE-UNDER-LYME Sutherland Arms(18) KENDAL Brewery Arts
Centre(19) OLDHAM Birch Hall Hotel,Lees(20) STAFFORD North
Staffs Polytechnic(21) WOLVERHAMPTON Lord Raglan(22)STEVENAGE
Gordon Craig Theatre(23) LONDON Dingwalls(24)BRIDGWATER Arts
Centre(25) SUNDERLAND Arts Centre(26) GLASGOW Third Eye
Centre(27) ABERDEEN University(28) ST ANDREWS University(29)
WEYBRIDGE College Of Food & Technology(June 1)and BIRMINGHAM
Polytechnic Westbourne Site(2).
We shall be re-promoting his Big Bear album"Gospel Wailing
Jazz Playing Rock'n'Rolling Soul Shouting Tap Dancing Bluesman
From New Orleans"(BEAR 3) to coincide with this tour.Following
this tour,Cousin Joe goes into the studios to record his 2nd
album for Big Bear.
NEW RELEASES due into the shops during the next 2 weeks are:

BEAR 11 "Boogie Piano-Chicago Style"   ERWIN HELFER
BEAR 12 "Johnny Mars & The Oakland Boogie" JOHNNY MARS

FRANCE

Big Bear Records are now being manufactured and distributed
in France by BASF(see attached Press Release).This makes a
total of 13 territories which take Big Bear with it's own
label identification - they are UK,Holland,Belgium,France,
Germany,Switzerland,Austria,Denmark,Sweden,Finland,Norway,
Australia & New Zealand.
Kind regards from myself and Kate to you and Betty.

JIM SIMPSON
js/cvm

**Max Jones was Melody Maker's top journalist, so he needed
to be kept informed of Cousin Joe's busy schedule.**

POST ⊞ OFFICE
No._____
OFFICE ST.
Charges to pay
£
RECEIVED

TELEGRAM
Prefix. Time handed in. Office of Origin and Service Instructions. Words.

At
To
By

⧾DA271 5.15 LONDON T 53

MR RICHARD NEWELL C/O BIG BEAR MUSIC 32 DEBLEN DRIVE
EDGBASTON-BHAM 16 =
CONGRATULATIONS ON THE THE SUCCESSFUL COMPLETION O
MARATHON TOUR. MANY THANKS FOR ALL YOUR HARD WORK
THE MANY TREMENDOUS PERFORMANCES. WISHING YOU GREAT
SUCCESS ON YOUR RETURN TO NORTH AMERICA =
LESLIE GOULD AND ALL AT FAMOUS MUSIC UK LTD +
C/O BIG BEAR 32 DEBLEN 16 TOUR PERFORMANCES. this form
GOULD UK LTD +   TSO .TGMS LN

**Richard Newell (aka The King Biscuit Boy) had just completed an
exhausting European tour from his Birmingham base**

Bash Street Blues Band at 'Enery's

Chapter 1
Home to great music

American Blues Legends 1975 and luxury coach Photo Jim Simpson

According to Chris Pitt, "most of my best memories revolved around Henry's, Tuesday's Bluesdays at the Crown. There were the blues legends like Arthur 'Big Boy' Crudup, Reverend Gary Davis, Lightnin' Slim, Eddie 'Guitar' Burns, Champion Jack Dupree, J.B. Hutto and Jimmy 'Fast Fingers' Dawkins. Then there were Thin Lizzy (saw them three times at Henry's), Pete Brown and Piblokto (also three times), Idle Race (twice), Duster Bennett, Barclay James Harvest, Medicine Head, The Dog that Bit People (I still have their album) and, of course, Brewer's Droop who must have acquired semi-resident status, so many times did I see them there. Who can forget Ron Watts belting out *I Can See Your Public Bar* with maybe a slight alteration to the last two words?"

Henry's Blueshouse, Birmingham's Home of the Blues, an early Big Bear project named after a particularly glamorous

... & SYMPHONY
... BLUESHOUSE,
... Hotel, Station Street.

TOMORROW (TUESDAY)
PALADIN PLUS ROAD
PALADIN PLUS ROAD
HENRY'S BLUESHOUSE
CROWN HOTEL, STATION STREET,
Behind New Street Station.
Only 25p. Open 7.30 p.m.
Wednesday: GERRY LOCKRAN.

HENRY'S BLUESHOUSE
Tomorrow — Sunday.
Everyone who caught the incredible
Brewer's Droop on their tour with Big
Boy Crudup will definitely be at
Henry's tomorrow. Those who have
missed Brewer's Droop are recom-
mended to listen to what we consider
to be the most entertaining and excit-
ing band in the country.
BREWER'S DROOP
CROWN HOTEL
Station Street,
(Behind New Street Station).
Open 7.30 p.m. Only 25p.
Tuesday—Trapeze.

TONIGHT
X-Colosseum and Mogul Thrash leader
James Litherland makes his first public
appearance with his new group Million.
JAMES LITHERLAND
& MILLION
HENRY'S BLUESHOUSE
CROWN HOTEL,
STATION STREET,
(behind New Street Station).
Open 7.30. Members 25p. Guests 30p.

TOMORROW — TUESDAY
PETE BROWN &
PIBLOKTO
HENRY'S BLUESHOUSE
Crown Hotel, Station Street (behind
New Street Station). Open 7.30 p.m.
Members 25p. Guests 30p.

TOMORROW (SUNDAY)
CAROL GRIMES
WITH UNCLE DOG
HENRY'S BLUESHOUSE
CROWN HOTEL
STATION STREET
(behind New Street Station)
Members 25p. Guests 30p.
Open 7.30 p.m.

TOMORROW — SUNDAY
PATTO — PATTO
HENRY'S BLUESHOUSE
CROWN HOTEL, STATION STREET
(Behind New Street Station).
Open 7.30. Members 25p. Guests 30p.

TOMORROW — TUESDAY
TRAPEZE
HENRY'S BLUESHOUSE
CROWN HOTEL, STATION STREET
(Behind New Street Station)
Members 25p. Guests 30p. Open 7.30.

TONIGHT
TRAPEZE
HENRY'S BLUESHOUSE
CROWN HOTEL, STATION STREET
(behind New Street Station). Members
25p. guests 30p. Open 7.30.

TOMORROW (SUNDAY)
MAN   MAN
HENRY'S BLUESHOUSE
CROWN HOTEL, STATION STREET
(Behind New Street Station). Members
25p. Guests 30p. Open 7.30 p.m.

TONIGHT AT HENRY'S
King of New Orleans Blues and Barrel-
house Piano.
CHAMPION JACK
DUPREE
plus
COLIN STAPLES BLUES BAND
HENRY'S BLUESHOUSE
Crown Hotel, Hill Street. (Behind New
Street Station).
Open 7.30. Members 30p Guests 40p
Sunday. Zoot Money.

TUESDAY AT HENRY'S
First ever public appearance of
ex-Bonzo
ROGER SPEAR
& HIS KINETIC WARDROBE
with
THUNDERCLAP NEWMAN
HENRY'S BLUESHOUSE
CROWN HOTEL, HILL STREET
(behind New St. Station)
OPEN 7.30
Bring your own trousers

TONIGHT
HENRY'S FOLK THING
CROWN HOTEL,
STATION STREET
(behind New Street Station).
Open 7.30.   Only 25p.
FLOOR ARTISTS WELCOME.

SUNDAY AT HENRY'S
All-time King Looner himself
ZOOT MONEY
ZOOT MONEY
Henry's Blueshouse,
Crown Hotel,
Hill Street (behind New Street Station)
Open 7.30 p.m.
Next Tuesday, Roger Spear plus
Thunderclap Newman.

TONIGHT AT HENRY'S
GASOLINE
PLUS
VILLAGE
HENRY'S BLUESHOUSE,
CROWN HOTEL,
STATION STREET
(Behind New Street Station).
Tickets on sale for American Blues
Festival, February 2.
Lightnin' Slim/J.B. Hutto/Eddie
Guitar Burns, 50p.

TUESDAY AT HENRY'S
GLEN CORNICK'S
WILD TURKEY
HENRY'S BLUESHOUSE,
CROWN HOTEL, STATION STREET
(Behind New Street Station)

TONIGHT AT HENRY'S
BEGGARS OPERA
HENRY'S BLUESHOUSE
CROWN HOTEL, STATION STREET
(Behind New Street Station).
Open 7.30.

TUESDAY AT HENRY'S
MIGHTY BABY
MIGHTY BABY
HENRY'S BLUESHOUSE,
CROWN HOTEL,
HILL STREET,
(behind New Street Station)
Open 7.30 p.m.

TOMORROW AT HENRY'S
BLONDE ON BLONDE
BLONDE ON BLONDE
HENRY'S BLUESHOUSE
Crown Hotel, Station Street.
(behind New Street Station)

TOMORROW — TUESDAY
GYPSY   GYPSY
HENRY'S BLUESHOUSE, CROWN
HOTEL, Station Street, (behind New
Street Station). Members 25p. Guests
30p. Open 7.30.

SUNDAY AT HENRYS
Donavans Backing Band
OPEN ROAD
OPEN ROAD
HENRY'S BLUES HOUSE
CROWN HOTEL
STATION STREET
(Behind NEW STREET STATION)
TUESDAY GYPSY

TONIGHT AT HENRY'S
PETE BROWN
& PIBLOKTO
HENRY'S BLUESHOUSE
CROWN HOTEL, Station Street, open
7.30. Sunday: The return of the
KING BISCUIT BOY

TUESDAY AT HENRY'S
First appearance on his first British
tour the legendary
KING BISCUIT BOY
The best mouth-harp player in the
world.
HENRY'S BLUESHOUSE
Crown Hotel, Station Street.
(Behind New Street Station)
Open 7.30 p.m.   Normal prices.

SUNDAY AT HENRY'S
Final British performance of the world's
greatest mouth-harp player:
KING BISCUIT BOY
plus
IDLE RACE
Henry's Blues House, Crown Hotel,
Station Street (behind New St. Station)
Normal prices. Come early.
Tuesday: Champion Jack Dupree.

TUESDAY AT HENRY'S
GASOLINE
PLUS
VILLAGE
HENRY'S BLUESHOUSE
CROWN HOTEL, STATION STREET
(behind New Street Station)
Tickets on sale for American Blues
Festival, February 2.
Lightnin' Slim/J.B. Hutto/
Eddie Guitar Burns
50p.

SUNDAY AT HENRY'S
GOOD HABIT
HENRY'S BLUESHOUSE,
CROWN HOTEL,
STATION STREET
(behind New Street Station)

SUNDAY AT HENRY'S
JUDE
(ex Procol Harum and Jethro Tull)
HENRY'S BLUES HOUSE,
CROWN HOTEL, STATION STREET
(behind New Street Station)

TOMORROW (SUNDAY)
From the musical Catch My Soul,
GASS   GASS
GASS   GASS
HENRY'S BLUESHOUSE
CROWN HOTEL, STATION STREET
(Behind New Street Station).
Members 25p.   Guests 30p
TUESDAY — GRACIOUS

TONIGHT AT HENRY'S
DANDO SHAFT
HENRY'S BLUESHOUSE,
CROWN HOTEL, STATION STREET
(behind New Street Station).

TUESDAY AT HENRY'S
44TH BIRTHDAY PARTY OF
AMERICAN BLUESMAN
EDDIE GUITAR BURNS
Henry's Blueshouse, Crown Hotel,
Station St. (behind New St. Station).
Normal prices.

TONIGHT
for all the people who could not get
in to see them last time we again
present
TRAPEZE
HENRY'S BLUESHOUSE
CROWN HOTEL,
STATION STREET
(Behind New Street Station).
Members 25p. Guests 30p.
Open 7.30 p.m.

SUNDAY AT HENRY'S
WARHORSE
HENRY'S BLUESHOUSE
CROWN HOTEL
STATION STREET
(Behind New Street Station)
Open 7.30.
Tuesday: BEGGARS OPERA.

TUESDAY AT HENRY'S
DANDO SHAFT
Henry's Blueshouse, Crown Hotel,
Station Street (behind New Street
Station).

SUNDAY AT HENRY'S
UFO   UFO
UFO   UFO
HENRY'S BLUESHOUSE,
CROWN HOTEL,
Station Street (behind New St. Station)
Tuesday: Lightnin' Slim.

TONIGHT at Henry's; Brewers
Droop.—Henry's Blueshouse, Crown
Hotel, Station Street; open 7.30.

TUESDAY AT HENRY'S
CAROL GRIMES & UNCLE DOG
PLUS SHY WOLF.
HENRY'S BLUESHOUSE, Crown Hotel,
Station Street (behind New
Station). Open 7.30 p.m.

SUNDAY HENRY'S
MARK ALMOND
MARK ALMOND
Henry's Blueshouse, Crown Hotel,
Station Street, open 7.30.
Tuesday: Brewers Droop.

SUNDAY AT HENRY'S
EX-BLOSSOM TOES
B. B. BLUNDER
HENRY'S BLUES HOUSE,
CROWN HOTEL,
STATION STREET
(behind New Street Station).

TONIGHT AT HENRY'S
Veteran Louisiana Bluesman
LIGHTNIN' SLIM
LIGHTNIN' SLIM
Henry's Blueshouse, Crown Hotel,
Station Street (behind New St. Station)

TUESDAY AT HENRY'S
Veteran Louisiana Bluesman
LIGHTNIN' SLIM
LIGHTNIN' SLIM
Henry's Blueshouse, Crown Hotel,
Station Street (behind New Street
Station).

JAZZ 'N' BLUES
SATURDAY, MARCH 4
FAREWELL APPEARANCE OF
LIGHTNIN' SLIM
veteran Louisiana Blues Man, 9-10
a.m. and Saratoga Jazz Band at
St. Philip's G.S.O.B.'s Club, Water-
works Road, Edgbaston, 8.30 p.m.
Come early. Members notice.

TONIGHT AT HENRY'S
JELLYBREAD
JELLYBREAD
HENRY'S BLUESHOUSE,
Crown Hotel, Station Street.

TONIGHT AT HENRY'S
BLONDE ON BLONDE
HENRY'S BLUESHOUSE
Crown Hotel, Station Street
(behind New St. Station)

SUNDAY AT HENRY'S
U.F.O.   U.F.O.
HENRY'S BLUESHOUSE
Crown Hotel, Station Street (behind
New Street Station) open 7.30 p.m.

TONIGHT AT HENRY'S
CAROL GRIMES &
UNCLE DOG
Plus Shy Wolf.
Henry's Blueshouse, Crown Hotel,
Station Street
(behind New Street Station)
Open 7.30 p.m.

TONIGHT AT HENRY'S
JELLY BREAD
JELLY BREAD
JELLY BREAD
JELLY BREAD
HENRY'S BLUESHOUSE,
CROWN HOTEL, STATION STREET
(behind New Street Station).
Open 7.30 p.m.

TUESDAY AT HENRY'S
JELLYBREAD
JELLYBREAD
Henry's Blueshouse, Crown Hotel,
Station Street.

TUESDAY AT HENRY'S
TEA & SYMPHONY
CHRISTMAS PARTY
With the fantastic Shuffling
Hungarians.
HENRY'S BLUESHOUSE,
CROWN HOTEL,
STATION STREET
(behind New Street Station)
Half price in fancy dress.

TONIGHT AT HENRY'S
King of New Orleans Blues and
Barrelhouse Piano.
CHAMPION JACK
DUPREE
plus the Pabanna.
Henry's Blueshouse, Crown Hotel,
Station Street. (Behind New Street
Station). Normal prices. Come early.

TOMORROW:
First ever appearance outside United
States of legendary Detroit Blues' Giant
EDDIE BURNS
who over the last 30 years has played
and recorded with such as Sonny Boy
Williamson and John Lee Hooker.
EDDIE GUITAR BURNS
Chess/Checker recording artist.
HENRY'S BLUES HOUSE, CROWN
HOTEL, STATION STREET.
Open 7.30 p.m.

Chicago bluesmen, with Birmingham's Bull Ring Centre as a backdrop Photo Jim Simpson

Afghan hound, had been a fixture in the upstairs room of the Crown in Station Street since 1968. From the outset it was full to capacity, with most of the audience happy to sit on the floor or dance to such bands as Status Quo, Thin Lizzy, Jethro Tull, Rory Gallagher and the like.

Henry's was famed not only for the roster of top British and American blues acts on offer, but as the place where Anthony Iommi and John Michael Osbourne, keen young punters, got to play the support spot with their new band. The time that Earth opened the show for Ten Years After was probably the most memorable of many memorable evenings at Henry's. The audience went crazy for those wild boys from Aston, so much so that they wouldn't let them leave the stage, insisting on encore after encore, to the obvious annoyance of TYA.

Renamed Black Sabbath, the band became Henry's regulars and went on to be managed by Henry's boss Jim Simpson who took them to two hit albums and one hit – and one miss – single. From their very first appearances the kids loved them. Not so the London-based record industry, nor the media. After 14 straight knockbacks from major recording companies their first release became a worldwide

> **The audience went crazy for those wild boys from Aston, so much so that they wouldn't let them leave the stage**

multi-million seller, but it was hardly welcomed by the music media! Today, of course, some 50 years later, they are revered as the original heroes of heavy metal and the godfathers of dozens of metal sub-styles.

As Simpson and the band took to the road and he had to abdicate some of his Henry's responsibilities, it was probably the beginning of the end for the club, but in the early 1970s Henry's was still flourishing.

Rose-Marie Smith has great memories of Henry's Blueshouse:

"I worked there as a barmaid and loved it there. My husband, Colin, was assistant manager to Tom Pickering and had worked at the Crown for a few years before we met. I worked there from 1970 to 1971 and then we moved on when we got our own pub."

April Phillips had great times there, too, from a slightly different perspective:

"My husband Nigel was in Tea and Symphony so we went to Henry's regularly."

Following the opening of Henry's was another legendary Birmingham club, Mothers, formerly the Carlton Ballroom and known as "the home of good sounds". Stephen Ward picks up the story:

"My favourite place in Birmingham in the early 1970s was Mothers in Erdington. Anyone who was anyone played there – even T Rex one time. It was such a modest place to attract the megastars."

Julia Rose remembers hearing Thunderclap Newman at Mothers and knowing instantly that *Love is in the Air* would be a hit – to most of us it came as a pleasant surprise! She also has impressive recall of the bands she heard at Mothers:

"Saw Pink Floyd, Jethro Tull, Free, Colosseum, Chick Corea, Family, Blodwyn Pig – whoever they were! All in the space of six months."

Stephen Ward was not wrong in describing Mothers as "a modest place". Above a furniture store in Erdington High Street, entered by a scruffy passageway, it was hardly luxurious for the punters, but that was nothing compared to the lot of musicians, humping gear up three flights of corrugated iron outside fire escape to the artists' entrance.

Nonetheless Phil Myatt, John Taylor and John Singer presided over many great nights at Mothers, among them performances by Chicago Transit Authority, later known worldwide as Chicago. Alan White of the website www.earlyblues.org, lists some 20-odd top bands that played there and sums up a few of the highspots, "Pink Floyd recorded *Ummagumma* at Mothers, The Who performed *Tommy* and Traffic staged their first gig."

Then there was the night that blues giant John Lee Hooker played Erdington. Such was the level of expectation that folk started to queue during the afternoon. Eventually there were nearly as many people outside, unable to get in, as there were inside. Backstage, where John Lee's dressing room was improvised in what normally served as the management office, all the seating had been removed to make space, leaving the star of the show spending his downtime sitting on the floor.

BRMB presenter Brian Savin with Cousin Joe from New Orleans Photo Jim Simpson

Though Mothers existed for less than three years, closing on January 3rd, 1971, it lives on in the occasional reference in song lyrics (Judas Priest's Rob Halford on his 2000 solo album *Resurrection*) or sleeve notes (for the album *The Canned Heat Cookbook*) and the remarkable tribute of being voted the world's best rock venue by *Billboard* magazine. Legendary DJ, the late John Peel, was quoted many years after Mothers closed as saying:

"I sometimes get mail from younger people who live in Erdington who are amazed to hear that for a few years the best club in Britain – and it was because I went to most of them – was right here in Birmingham."

After Henry's closed, a sort of shadow club, 'Enery's, operated briefly, but by the end of 1972 both Henry's and Mothers were no more. As Stephen Ward commented, "All that's left of Mothers is a blue plaque and memories."

> **After Henry's closed, a sort of shadow club, Enery's, operated briefly, but by the end of 1972 both Henry's and Mothers were no more.**

The Crown meanwhile, battered and boarded up, now forms a derelict contrast to the shiny new Grand Central complex. "Heard some great bands there in the early seventies. It's a crime that it's in its current state," is how Nigel Smith sums it up.

Henry's Blueshouse, however, has taken on new life for the 21st century, recently revived in the upstairs room of a pub (what else?), this time the Bull's Head in Bishopsgate Street, then, after that pub's closure, at the Velvet Music Rooms.

Somewhere...

Under the Rainbow Suite were the Co-op and British Home Stores in High Street. However, access was a bit classier than getting into Mothers: there was even a lift, plus a doorman called Tiny – he was huge! Doug Thompson started the venue in the mid-60s, but after his untimely demise in a particularly nasty industrial accident in 1968, his brother Brian took over, presiding over an entertainment empire that also included the Mayfair Suite and the Cinephone cinema among other things.

Musically the policy went through various changes, with appearances by Robert Plant, the Rockin' Berries and the Walker Brothers among others, but for some time the resident band was The Craig, with Carl Palmer, later of Emerson, Lake and Palmer, on drums. According to Rob Martin, on Saturday nights in the early 1970s, the music was "reggae and stuff", while Christine Fox sums up the Rainbow's appeal neatly:

Musically the policy went through various changes, with appearances by Robert Plant, the Rockin' Berries and the Walker Brothers among others

---

"It was very dark in there; the music was loud, but good!"

Matthew Edwards remembers it as "a great space" and many have fond memories of the roof top space, high above Birmingham's High Street, though Christine Fox introduces a touch of dour reality:

'The roof top would never be allowed now.'

Maybe Health and Safety could get round to it after sorting out the vertiginous fire escape at Mothers!

The Rainbow Suite outlasted the 1970s, giving scope for many memories, none more personal than Stephen Ward's:

"I was in love with the girl in the cloakroom. She was gorgeous – danced like a dream!"

If you were that gorgeous girl in the cloakroom, let us know!

Blues city UK

Ask anyone in Birmingham what the blues means to them and most people will have something to say about the football at St. Andrew's, but in the 1970s Birmingham (that's Birmingham, England, not Alabama) could lay claim to be being home to a very different sort of blues.

Where else in the country could you happen into a bar, hotel or music store and find yourself next to Lightnin' Slim, the Louisiana King of Swamp Blues, Doctor Ross the Harmonica Boss the partly crazy one-man-band from Tunica, Mississippi (who knew Elvis, but remembered him as Elvis Preston, a nice kid who drove a truck), or Tommy Tucker who, a decade earlier, had the world dancing to his hit, *High Heel Sneakers?*

Over the decade some 30 American bluesmen made Birmingham their temporary home, their base for UK and European tours which lasted for six or seven weeks and which were organised by Birmingham agency, Big Bear Music. And for Birmingham musicians and audiences the benefits were considerable and sometimes unexpected. Of course the city was on the tour schedules, but, on their nights off, what should the bluesmen do but gig at Birmingham pubs and clubs? The Brummie blues fan had the chance to get to know informally some of the wildest and most eccentric of authentic American bluesmen.

In 1973, for instance, Digbeth Civic Hall hosted both The American Blues Legends 73 and the 1973 Chicago Blues Festival with such colourful characters as Homesick James, One Arm John Wrencher, Eddie Playboy Taylor, Boogie Woogie Red and Washboard Willie.

AMERICAN BLUES LEGENDS '75
HOMESICK JAMES - TOMMY TUCKER - BILLY BOY ARNOLD - LITTLE JOE BLUE - EDDIE GUITAR BURNS - LONESOME JIMMIE - LEE ROBINSON and drummer PETE YORK.
SATURDAY 10th MAY 7.45 p.m.
DIGBETH CIVIC HALL, BIRMINGHAM
(2 mins walk New St. Station & Bull Ring Centre) Tickets £1. Town Hall Box Office. Enquiries Big bear Records 021-454 7020

Page 48—MELODY MAKER, May 10, 1975

Chapter 2
Give my regards to Broad Street

Broad Street was once home to an array of upmarket car showrooms, the BBC in Birmingham and the city's main exhibition centre, an important thoroughfare and the main route west out of the City Centre. By the 1970s Broad Street was changing fast, rather less dignified than it had been, but definitely more fun.

Some elements of the old Broad Street were still there in the 1970s. The elegant gardens of the Hall of Memory remained, as did Bingley Hall. This had been the prime exhibition venue in Birmingham for many years, but the opening of the National Exhibition

A GUIDE TO BROAD STREET AREA 1970s STYLE	
NIGHTCLUBS	**RESTAURANT**
Bakers	Flower Drum
Barbarella's	
Burberries	**PUBS**
Faces	The Crown
Martin's Room	The Granville
Mr. Moons	The Prince of Wales
The Opposite Lock	
The Rum Runner	**CAFES**
BALLROOM	Rendezvous
The West End	The Tow Rope
	Venus

"When we had finished our set and returned to the dressing room, Michael and his brothers were having a prayer meeting before going on stage. I should say that Michael was amazing. He had just started recording *Off the Wall* and his immense talent was obvious. He was also down to earth and always spoke to us.

"For the first show in Brighton they had a huge stage set created out of clear perspex lit from below with coloured lights. They also had a massive fibre-optic peacock in a frame which stood at the back of the stage. However, after the fourth gig, most of the perspex sheets had warped with the heat, meaning they didn't lie flat, causing no end of problems when the brothers tried to dance. And the peacock was too big to fit into most of the theatres. Needless to say, none of this made its way to Bingley Hall!"

Adjacent to Bingley Hall, theatre came back to Broad Street for the first time since the Prince of Wales Theatre took a direct hit from a German bomb in 1941. Now the Repertory Theatre moved in after 58 years on Station Street.

> **Some elements of the old Broad Street were still there in the 1970s. The elegant gardens of the Hall of Memory remained, as did Bingley Hall**

Centre in 1976 stole its thunder and it seemed shabbier and less relevant. A few years later a major fire during the Midland Caravan, Camping and Leisure Exhibition in 1984 destroyed the building and the demolition crews moved in.

Even as late as 1979 Bingley Hall had its moments of glory. Des Tong has great memories of playing there in a band called The Dougie James Soul Train in support of Michael Jackson on his *Destiny* tour. The tour took in three continents and nine countries and finished in Hawaii in January 1980, but on a cold, snowy night in February it was the turn of Bingley Hall. As Des relates:

"The first thing we found was that there was only one dressing room, but, as we'd already played Brighton, Preston, Glasgow and Manchester, they seemed to like us, even though we were extremely zany and I'm not sure they 'got' us. We would do things like stop in the middle of a song and all tell a joke in unison, then carry on as if nothing had happened. Always smack on the beat! However, they welcomed us into the huge room at the back of the stage and we occupied one corner and they the other.

DEREK RAWDEN and JEFFREY S. KRUGER Present

The JACKSONS

...'THE FIRST FAMILY OF SOUL'...

THE BRIGHTON CENTRE, BRIGHTON. SATURDAY, FEBRUARY 10, at 9.00 p.m.
Tickets: £5; £4; £3. Available from Box Office. Tel. (0273) 202881
THE GUILDHALL, PRESTON. SUNDAY FEBRUARY 11, at 8.45 p.m. Tickets:
£5; £4; £3. Available from Box Office. Tel. (0772) 21721.
THE FIESTA CLUB, SHEFFIELD. TUESDAY, FEBRUARY 13.
THE APOLLO THEATRE, GLASGOW. FRIDAY, FEBRUARY 16, at 9.15 p.m.
Tickets: £5; £4; £3. Available from Box Office. Tel. (041) 332-9221.
THE APOLLO THEATRE, MANCHESTER. SATURDAY, FEBRUARY 17, at 9.15
p.m. Tickets: £5; £4; £3. Available from Box Office. Tel. (061) 273-1112.
THE BINGLEY HALL, BIRMINGHAM. SUNDAY, FEBRUARY 18, at 8.15 p.m.
Tickets: £5 on the night. £4 in advance. Available from Box Office
THE CIVIC THEATRE, HALIFAX. MONDAY, FEBRUARY 19, at 6.45 p.m. and
9.15 p.m.
THE DE MONTFORT HALL, LEICESTER. TUESDAY, FEBRUARY 20, at 9.15 p.m.
Tickets: £5; £4; £3. Available from Box Office. Tel. (0533) 27632
THE SOPHIA GARDENS PAVILION, CARDIFF. WEDNESDAY, FEBRUARY 21,
at 9.15 p.m. Tickets: £5; £4.50; £4; £3.50; £3. Available from Box Office.

**The massed ranks of Big Bear Ffolly
– how many can you recognise?**

Lee Longlands, a reminder of a more dignified Broad Street

Broad Street seventies-style was no longer home to the BBC which had decamped to Carpenter Road, George Clay's music shop carried on into the 1970s, but the huge windows of the car showrooms were empty. The Art Deco façade of Lee Longlands furniture store, the great survivor of Broad Street, remained in splendid isolation.

But the early seeds of today's bustling entertainment centre were there as night clubs flourished on Broad Street. Barbarella's, one of several fun palaces in Eddie Fewtrell's club empire (and one of the few not named after one of the King of Clubs' daughters!), was an early arrival on the scene. Barbarella's was on Cumberland Street, two minutes stroll from the main thoroughfare.

John O'Hara's claims to fame include building what were then the largest curved advertising boards in Europe on the corner of Broad Street and Ryland Street. He is an excellent guide to the progress of the transformation of Broad Street in the 1970s (with a few asides about the street's pubs):

"I don't think the Brasshouse was converted from the old Weights and Measures building until the 1980s or even the 1990s. What's now O'Neills was definitely the Granville which I called the Westward Ho after the name of the lounge at the back. The Crown was a very popular pub with the large lounge catering for the office workers and younger people, with the bar being more for the older people (Mary served behind the bar. She was top drawer – had your drink ready before you reached the bar). The old BBC studio used to be near the Rum Runner and there was a Chinese restaurant almost opposite Sheepcote Street called the Flower Drum.

"The Orthopaedic Hospital, later Old Orleans among other names, was still there in the seventies and I remember the Oxfam shop next to it. There was a dance hall at the top end of Broad Street, possibly Suffolk Street, called the West End. There were cobblestones leading up to it – it probably closed in the early seventies – and there was also a café opposite Bingley Hall called the Venus – I can remember my sisters going for a frothy coffee in the fifties with their pleated skirts and white ankle socks."

Probably the most cunningly named night club in Birmingham was The Opposite Lock, a short stroll from Broad Street down Gas Street. If not precisely opposite a lock, it was certainly alongside the canal, maybe all of six feet

away. Owner Martin Hone had some form as a racing driver, a sport in which apparently the term "applying opposite lock" is common currency. The club was fairly upmarket, though a strangely rambling affair, converted from an old factory building and spreading over two and a half floors. The décor left no doubt of who the owner was, Martin Hone's beaming face appearing in multiple photographs all round the walls. Just in case you missed the point, the club's members' room went under the name of Martin's Room, a much posher large lounge with chesterfields that could swallow up a small person.

The Lock was a frequent destination for the more discerning clubber, but what made it stand out from other niteries was its music. Martin Hone's favourite act was American lounge and jazz singer Marion Montgomery who was a regular visitor, but the smart money on what was the most memorable performance there was on the night that Basie came to The Lock. The Count Basie Orchestra – all 16 of them – played to an overflowing capacity audience of maybe 250 people, some of the lucky ones only some three feet from the most swinging big band in jazz.

At the other extreme, equally memorable in its own way, was the January 1970 appearance of the Big Bear Ffolly, a showcase for bands managed by the Birmingham company. After Locomotive, of *Rudi's in Love* fame, Tamworth

---

Alongside what had been the home of the BBC, with its quaint cobbled hill sloping down to the canal, the Rum Runner was a niterie famed for its live music

---

blues band Bakerloo and the nutty Moseley combo Tea & Symphony, there, on the bottom of the bill was the emerging Black Sabbath, with the classic original line-up, Ozzy, Tony, Geezer and Bill.

Close to what had been the home of the BBC, with its quaint cobbled hill sloping down to the canal, the Rum Runner was a niterie famed for its live music, cool DJs and celebrity clients such as Roy Wood and members of Black Sabbath and Led Zeppelin. Tony Iommi recalled:

'I used to go up Broad Street all the time with my mate John Bonham. The Rum Runner's owner was a pal of ours.'

Originally a casino, the Rum Runner was undoubtedly one of the stars of Broad Street. It reopened as a full-blown niterie in the early 1970s, featuring good live music. The first house band was Magnum and, when they went on the road, attractions included Quill and Jigsaw. Around about 1978 Paul and Michael Berrow, sons of the club's founder, came back from a visit to Studio 54 in New York, ready to transform the Rum Runner. At the same time the then unknown Duran Duran brought in a demo, hoping to be booked for the club. Instead they were offered rehearsal space and jobs at the club: Roger Taylor as a glass collector, Andy Taylor as a cook, John Taylor as doorman and Nick Rhodes as club DJ. Unsurprisingly Duran Duran became the club's resident band, the Berrow Brothers became their managers and fame beckoned.

27

The Tow Rope, last resort of Broad Street's Dirty Stop Outs

And that name? Nothing to do with the famed Panamanian boxer – it's back to the movies! The band also crossed Broad Street to play Barbarella's, so naturally they named themselves after the evil scientist, Durand Durand, in the film *Barbarella* – what else?

Josep Behan remembers going to a beach party at the Rum Runner – do canals have beaches? – but what next when even the night clubs close? The Tow Rope all-night café has left indelible memories – and not just for the food:

"It was the place to crash after Rum Runner." (Wilf Hobart)

"Spent many hours in here for breakfast after the Cedar Club, etc." (Sue Fear)

"The Tow Rope was a great finisher after a night at Barbarella's. You could see all sides of life here there while stuffing your face with a full English." (Andrew Harris)

Pete King is more explicit on the "all sides of life" on show at the Tow Rope:

"Me and my mates were so young. We used to tell our folks we were staying at a friend's and a few of us would hang around in town and wind up at the Tow Rope. Pure delinquency! Lots of bad stuff going on which was great and led us astray! You could hear the pills rolling across the table tops."

Terry Poole of Bakerloo was another to enjoy the all-night breakfasts:

"Mugs of tea at 5 am and fried egg sandwiches. All sorts in there, including me – a young musician!"

So was the food great? How about Michelin stars? Andrew Harris has his doubts:

"Michelin stars? I reckon their sausages were made out of Michelin tyres."

Night out with an elephant

Up towards Five Ways, where the Park Regis Hotel now stands, were two clubs, Faces and Baker's. Co-author of this book, Jim Simpson, has a memory of an event at Faces (or was it Baker's?) so bizarre and so blurred in detail that it might almost have been a dream.

Working at the time in music promotion, management and recording, he was called on for some odd tasks, such as hosting a beauty contest at Baker's (or was it Faces?). Perhaps it wasn't so strange to find the winner parading round the club in a swim suit far from the beach in the middle of the night, but that she did so on the back of an elephant made this a night to remember. Or perhaps to forget! After some 45 years we can't find anyone else who remembers the event.

Perhaps it was such a matter of routine that Broad Streeters took it in their stride. Jim remembers clearly that the crowd at Faces (or was it Baker's?) was nonchalant about the whole thing so long as the elephant didn't block the way to the bar.

Note for zoologists: Jim is convinced that it was an Indian elephant, not an African, which at least saved the winner a 10-foot climb!

Jim Simpson as beauty contest MC, but who were the contestants? And was this the occasion when the elephant was in the room?

Barbarella's, looking less than glamorous

Chapter 3
King of clubs

In 1970s Birmingham the name Eddie Fewtrell was synonymous with night clubs. Rejoicing in his nickname, "The king of clubs", Eddie owned and operated more night clubs sited in choice locations than you could shake a stick at – well, to be more precise, by 1979 he owned eight clubs and bars. His original Cedar Club on Constitution Hill kicked things off in 1965, but by the seventies he had a string of clubs, several of them named after his daughters: Abigail's or the 3,000 capacity Rebecca's, later rebranded as Boogies.

Later editions included the upstairs/downstairs Edward's Number 7 and Number 8, but for hardcore club and disco fans, Barbarella's on Cumberland Street, just off Broad Street, was the must-go-to. A host of top bands appeared at Barbarella's – incidentally not named after a Fewtrell daughter, but Jane Fonda's sexy space traveller in the 1968 film. Imagine seeing, close up in a club atmosphere, such acts as The Ramones, AC/DC, Dr. John or Ike and Tina Turner!

One memorable night Chuck Berry appeared at Barbarella's, but, of course, Chuck being Chuck, there was a problem

In the early 1970s Des Tong was the bass player/MD for a Liverpool vocal group called The Chants. He recalls playing Barbarella's:

"We performed all over the UK and Europe and in 1971 we were booked to appear at Barbarella's for a week (yes, a week!) as support to The Four Tops. Expecting it to be a group of sound-alikes, we arrived on the Sunday to find it was the real Four Tops, Levi Stubbs and all.

"We had enrolled a drummer friend of mine from Manchester, but struggled to find a good keyboard player. Imagine then our surprise when we discovered a fabulous pianist Mike Alexander playing in the Take Two room. A deal was struck and every night minus his bow-tie Mike would join us on Fender Rhodes for the Chants set. It was a great week, most nights ending with a trip to the Tow Rope for the all-night breakfast."

One memorable night Chuck Berry appeared at Barbarella's, but, of course, Chuck being Chuck, there was a problem. Just 45 minutes into a scheduled 75 minute performance, with the crowd going wild, he marched offstage, straight out of the stage door and into his waiting rented limousine. Chuck sat in the back seat, calmly smoking, while the duty manager knocked on the car window, begging Chuck to get back on stage and rejoin his backing band who

BARBARELLA'S
41 CUMBERLAND STREET
BIRMINGHAM 1

2nd Feb – TALKING HEADS
3rd Feb – ROBERT GORDON
4th Feb – ULTRAVOX
7th Feb – DRONES
9th Feb – SQUEEZE
10th Feb – TYLA GANG
11th Feb – THE BOYS
14th Feb – SUPERCHARGE
17th Feb – DAMNED
18th Feb – XTC
21st Feb – ADVERTS
24th Feb – EARTHQUAKE
25th Feb – ZAL
28th Feb – BLONDIE

Present this Ad any Sunday Night
For Free Admission

barbarella's
41 CUMBERLAND ST. BIRMINGHAM B1 2JA
Sunday, 9th October, 1977
IN CONCERT
Miss Spent Youth
DOORS OPEN 8.00 p.m.
THIS TICKET ADMITS TWO
NOT VALID AFTER 10.00 p.m.
DRINKS - LAGER & BREAKERS 40p
All other drinks
　　　BEER, VODKA, SPIRITS 35p
N⁰ 931
Upon entry 50p will be charged, the full
50p is redeemable at the bar for drinks

Cannon Hill

MUSIC
The Arthur Doyle Concert Band
15 April 7.30 p.m.

Flutes, Reeds & Whistles — Music Studio
17 April 10.00 a.m. & 2.00 p.m.
Frances Eager — Piano
19 April 7.30 p.m.

THEATRE
National Youth Theatre in

FAMILY TIES

A double bill by Peter Terson

Wrong first time
Never right, yet again

3 - 8 April 7.30 p.m. — 8 April 2.30 p.m.

LECTURE
Birmingham's Posh Areas in the last 100 years.
11 April 7.30 p.m.
Box Office 021 - 440 3838.

OPEN DOOR

counselling service
for young people
free and confidential

Walk in 6.00 to 8.30 p.m. Mondays,
Tuesdays, Thursdays and Fridays.,
Carrs Lane Counselling Centre,
Carrs Lane (alongside Marks and Spencers)
Phone: 021 643 - 7717 (Weekday mornings).

barbarella's
41, Cumberland St
Birmingham, 1
643 9413/4/5/6

Top rock bands, live, on stage
top-line entertainment
all week

April

X-RAY SPECS 11

ELVIS COSTELLO ...13 & 14

THE PLEASERS .... 21 & 22

SIOUXSIE & THE BANSHEES 25

RICKY COOL & 28
THE ICEBURGS .. & 29

FREE ADMISSION
into Barbarella's on Sundays
with this advert. 50p will be
charged at the door but is
refundable at the bar.

643 4544
rebecca's
7, Severn St, Birmingham centre

Black Slate............7

Tapper Zukie......10

Steve Jones of the Sex Pistols at Barbarella's

were carrying on regardless, almost ignored by the audience. It soon became obvious that Chuck wanted an additional 500 pounds cash on top of his contracted fee. Given a choice between finding the cash and seeing the irate crowd smash up the room, the manager scurried round emptying the tills and Chuck Berry completed a stunning set!

Ask Brummie Dirty Stop Outs of a certain vintage their favourite bands at Barbarella's and the list seems endless (see *The Official Dirty Stop Out's Guide to Bands at Barbarella's*). Some may protest, Chico White claiming to be 'probably too drunk' (surely not, Chico!) and Robin Westley Martin waxing mightily indignant:

"How on earth can I be expected to remember anything about going to Barb's or what went on there, for Goodness' sake?"

But most responded with a flood of names from the most famous to the now totally obscure, Kay Medlock asking optimistically if anyone remembers 'a band called o'. Little Acre was a popular choice, pioneers of blue-eyed soul, nearly-made-its whose chances of national success were hampered by a floating line-up of up to ten – not good for clubs with small stages and small budgets!

Close-up encounters with the famous in the club atmosphere are still remembered 40-plus years later. Paul Harris "bought Sylvain Sylvain a pint at the David Johanssen gig" and complains about Mick Jones of the Clash being miserable (was it something you said?). For triple name-dropping Maggie O'Connell deserves some sort of award:

"I remember standing at the bar with Ian Dury talking to Steve Gibbons about Wreckless Eric."

Then there was Iggy Pop, coming out in a boxer's dressing gown and gloves, according to Matt Edwards. "Did he have see-through kecks on?," enquired Paul Harris. "I'm not sure about his trousers," replied Matt which suggests that this time they weren't see-through!

Wilf Hobart's happiest memory of Barbarella's was seeing Ian Dury and the Blockheads there – then, as an afterthought, "Oh, yes, and meeting my wife!"

Edited: Derek Johnson

IGGY POP GIGS

THE NOTORIOUS Iggy Pop arrives in Britain at the end of this month for a five-week tour, and an extensive itinerary is at present being lined up for him. The greater part of his schedule has not yet been finalised, and it is expected that the majority of his dates will be confirmed within the next week or two. Nine venues are, however, already definite and these are:

London Kensington Biba's Restaurant (April 30 and May 1), Malvern Winter Gardens (May 3), Loughborough University (4), Norwich Theatre Royal (6), Northwich Memorial Hall (8), Birmingham Barbarella's (21), Cleethorpes Winter Gardens (23), Manchester Stoneground (24) and Leeds Playhouse Theatre (June 3).

Iggy — whose current CBS album is "Raw Power", mixed by David Bowie — is also expected to appear on television during his visit, probably in BBC-2's "Old

Roxy date switch

ROXY MUSIC's two "secret" concerts at Southport Floral Hall, plans for which were exclusively revealed in last week's NME, will now take place next Tuesday and Wednesday (9 and 10) — and not today and tomorrow (4 and 5) as originally announced by the venue's management. As reported, Roxy have planned the dates as a warm-up for their forthcoming U.S. tour. Tuesday's gig is already sold out, but at press-time there were still

Birmingham's Dirty Stop Outs had warning of Iggy Pop's excesses!

Renowned Dirty Stop Out Brian the Tooth with blues singer Roy Everett and his wife Dot

OFFICIAL DIRTY STOP OUT'S GUIDE TO BANDS AT BARBARELLA'S – TOP 20

- The Clash
- Wire
- Blondie
- The Damned
- Iggy Pop
- David Johansen Band
- Elvis Costello
- Dr. Feelgood
- Talking Heads
- Heavy Metal Kids
- Little Acre
- Magazine
- X Ray Spex
- Only One
- The Killjoys
- Ian Dury and the Blockheads
- Ike and Tina Turner
- Bebop De Luxe
- Freddie King
- Commander Cody and his Lost Planet Airmen

Rebecca's, recalls Jim Cronin, "was on three floors: cool and jazz upstairs, chart music on the ground floor and funk and soul in the basement. And you could buy your *Sunday Mercury* at the door as you left at 2.00 am after a Saturday night." Good place to work, too – Tony Smith used to work there "collecting glasses and meeting girls" – that's what you call a job spec!

The long staircase at Rebecca's figures in the story of Terry the Toupe, a larger than life character despite his diminutive stature, forever hanging out with bands and even driving the braver ones to gigs. Terry was a spectacular dancer, as fit as a flea with the courage of a lion. What he wasn't was nattily attired. This, combined with his carrot-coloured toupee, not always quite straight, made him less than popular as classier clubs like Rebecca's.

So there he was, bounding up the staircase with dancing on his mind, only to be told by the two heavies on the door that he wasn't welcome and should try elsewhere, maybe somewhere less smart. Of course Terry protested and one of the bouncers thought he would be cute, snatched the toupee

from Terry's head and tossed it towards the door. There it sat halfway down the stairs, leaving its owner scratching his naked pate and figuring his next move. Suddenly he bounded down the stairs, carefully, almost ceremoniously, placed the toupee where it belonged, and ran back up to confront the pair of bouncers. He whacked the first and laid out the second at which the first staggered to his feet and ran into the club.

So Terry the Toupe, pride and toupee both restored, strolled into the club and was soon on the dance floor, watched balefully by the surviving doorman – from a safe distance, of course.

Eddie Fewtrell, regularly photographed with such stars as Smokin' Joe Frazier and Tom Jones, a regular act at Eddie's venues, enjoyed his celebrity, but came from a humble background, one of ten children born and brought up in a broken home in one of the less grand parts of Aston. From an early age Eddie was the family breadwinner and soon developed a name as a hard man. He always seemed to relish his reputation on the fringe of the underworld, recounting with obvious pride his successful Battle of Snow Hill in the 1960s when he fought off the challenge of the Kray and Richardson gangs to his home territory. The authorised version appeared in his book, *The King of Clubs*, and Eddie was distinctly displeased when daughter Abigail supplied her husband, David Keogh, with the material for a revised version in *The Accidental Gangster,* and then had the temerity to pen a novel on the same theme!

Not all Birmingham night spots were part of the Fewtrell empire, though it must have seemed so at times. By the 1970s, for instance, the Elbow Room, adjacent to the Aston Hippodrome and the historic pub the Barton's Arms, was well established as the hangout for Brum's musicians. It was treated by them as a social club on their nights off and as the place to get an after-hours drink and a bite to eat on the return from an out-of-town gig. Many's the band that spent the last mile of the drive back, trundling along in their invariably battered van, in happy anticipation of Frank the Yank's legendary toasted steak sandwiches at the Elbow.

John Parsons had over 14 years built the Belfry into a force to be reckoned with, presenting top bands at weekends, when he bought the Elbow Room and set about booking some interesting bands. His pal, Steve Winwood, by then a

---

So Terry the Toupe, pride and toupee both restored, strolled into the club and was soon on the dance floor, watched balefully by the surviving doorman

---

substantial big venue box-office draw, appeared at the Elbow Room, but John's biggest coup was probably to present the chart-topping Kinks at the club. He booked them into the Belfry on a double, that is, two shows in different venues on the same night. Clearly his friendship with the band was an important factor, but this might just rate as the coolest ever Birmingham night club booking: a small fee, food and drink.

Bands were formed in that small, but uber-cool, niterie, recording plans hatched and occasionally a musician would be informed that his services were no longer required. Because it was such a musician-friendly venue, bands were always pleased to perform there, whatever the fee. Bands like nothing more than playing for other musicians,

but there was a downside for any band that featured a Hammond organ. Hoisting a B3 up those steep narrow stairs, negotiating that tight halfway bend, was almost enough to dampen anyone's spirit. Almost.

There was, however, at least one night when any musician in town would have been delighted to haul up the Animal, as the B3 Hammond was known. That was the night that the legendary New Orleans piano player and singer, Dr. John, appeared in that tiny room. The good doctor was going through a low period at the time, both with regard to his health and his career. Amazingly he was staying temporarily in Edgbaston and playing a few shows around the city because he needed the money. Elbow Room owner, Albert Chapman, naturally enough, has fond memories of the evening. The Junction in Harborne was another place to benefit from having the Night Tripper on the doorstep.

And the Elbow Room made its mark far beyond Aston. John Parsons, former band manager, club and pub owner and very much a Brum man-about-music, was never short of quirky ideas. In due course he opened a sister night club to the Elbow in Spain. Called El Codo (Spanish for The Elbow, naturally), it occupied a desirable spot, virtually beach-side in the Los Boliches district of Fuengirola.

The end for Sloopy's

The director of Sloopy's niterie on Corporation Street was arraigned at the Magistrates Court, just across the street from the club, on a charge of not only allowing drunkenness on his premises, but also of insisting on it! Following police objections, he decided not to renew his licence and closed down Sloopy's.

Could that be a notice of closure on Sloopy's door?

Cousin Joe at the
Elbow Room with
co-owners David
Postle and Albert
Chapman, later
manager of Black
Sabbath

Chapter 4
A Touch of the romantics

Come the mid-seventies, there started a steadily increasing stream of strangely attired young folk making their way down Hurst Street. They were, the cognoscenti informed us, new romantics. Egyptian queens rubbed heavily padded shoulders with ancient Babylonians, girly pirates and dashing highwaymen. Their destination was the home of that celebrated pair of designers pretty much responsible for the new romantic look, Mesdames Kahn and Bell. They created the look of many notable bands who supplied the soundtrack to the new romantic movement, including the high priests, Duran Duran. Interestingly, Simon Le Bon wrote the Duranies' song *Kahnada* about Jane Kahn. Their designs were elaborate and theatrical, with influences from Egyptian, African and Far Eastern art, always futuristic and often beyond the realms of fantasy, and there's no denying that Patti Bell and Jane Kahn were the high priestesses of the nationwide new romantics look.

> ## Egyptian queens rubbed heavily padded shoulders with ancient Babylonians, girly pirates and dashing highwaymen

They didn't get the recognition they deserved in some quarters – London, actually – particularly when London-based designers started to copy the Kahn and Bell look, with many experts preferring to suggest that London's luvvies had actually been copied by Birmingham's finest.

A decade later *Blueprint* summed up the appeal of Kahn & Bell in prose almost as exotic as their creations:

"Kahn and Bell had particular impact. Holding court at the Zanzibar, resplendent in leopardskin and padded shoulders, dripping diamonte with leather devils' tails hanging down between their legs, they looked on good nights like Egyptian queens, like ancient Babylonians. On not so good nights, they resembled Brassai's Moma Bijou – 'fugitives from Baudelaire's bad dreams', and even then they looked magnificent. For Kahn and Bell and those who followed their lead, identity wasn't something you nailed yourself into in late adolescence. It was a trick of the light and if you were to avoid burning yourself out (a real risk this, when you sold clothes all day and promoted them all night), then you simply let the flames lick over you and turned the ashes into kohl."

Jane and Patti split in the 1980s, with the former relocating to London and Patti Bell staying firmly in Birmingham, with her inspired, thought-provoking fashions in demand throughout Europe, South East Asia and Japan.

Formality in dress lingered in the 1970s – you wouldn't get politicians appeared tie-less on television – but the exotic and the eccentric were making a growing impact. For instance, Martin Degville, a teenage designer and aspiring fashion icon from Walsall, ran Degville's Dispensary in Birmingham with the aid of his flatmate. Dave Ward tells the tale:

"Martin had a shop downstairs in the Oasis next to the café in 1977/78. He had some weird and wonderful clothes and Boy George moved here from Liverpool and worked in the shop occasionally. Martin went on to form Sigue Sigue Sputnik – I don't know what happened to George..."

According to Dave, Martin and George also ran Bowie and Roxy Nights at the Top Rank from time to time – there's one for the "Before they were famous" file!

The popular place for the latest in male fashions was Nelson House which had shops in Dale End and in the underpass leading to The Bull Ring. Known for up-to-date fashions, they also boasted that they did a roaring trade in 1950s teddy boy clothing. One customer remarked of their clothing, "It was only made to be worn once because the first time it was washed it either shrank or lost all semblance of shape." He remained a regular customer! No doubt a comment on the rapidity of fashion change in the 1970s, one wearing, out of date, one wash, out of shape!

The Mayfair Suite, labelled "a weird place" by one punter

Mayfair Suite
BIRMINGHAM

DINING • DANCING
☆☆ **CABARET** ☆☆
EVERY SATURDAY
Commencing February 5th.

The Sensation of '**77**

SAMPLE MENU
Coupe Hawaiian
(Cocktail of Pineapple, Orange & Grapefruit)

Entrecote Chasseur
(Grilled Sirloin Steak
with a Sauce of Mushrooms
Tomatoes, Tarragon & White Wine)

**Selection of
Seasonable Vegetables**

Gateaux Foret Noir
(Chocolate & Cherry Gateaux)

Chocolat Menthe Cafe
(Coffee & Mints)

8 P.M - 1 A.M.
CABARET 10·30 p.m.
Table reservations for
diners ring 021-643 2137

ENJOY A SUPERB
EVENING AT THE
MAYFAIR SUITE
WITH A
SPECIALLY SELECTED
☆ **4 Course Dinner**
☆ **Cabaret**
☆ **Non-Stop Dancing**
☆ **Resident Band**
☆ **Resident Group**
For only

£3 Per Head FULLY INCLUSIVE
MIN-AGE 18
Non-Diners welcome
ADMISSION AT THE DOOR £1
Special party rate for 50 or more persons.
MECCA *of course!*

High fashion at Birmingham Beauty Contest

Music at the Mayfair

The Mayfair Suite adjacent to New Street Station is the source of many different happy memories, with such bands as Siouxsie and the Banshees, Canned Heat and Human League figuring largely in Mayfair-goers' memories. Robin Westley Martin "used to go to a dance every Sunday with Brian T the DJ – there were two rooms inside, The Mayfair Suite and The Prince Charles Suite", but he also recalls all-nighters with Hawkwind and Alice Cooper.

Paul Weston went to The Mayfair for a quite different brand of music:

"I went to plenty of fabulous reggae evenings in the early 1970s. I still am a reggae fan. In those days I used to get my records from Don Christie's in Ladypool Road."

David Hadley rather unfairly labels The Mayfair Suite "a weird place" on the strength of one odd happening:

"I saw Atomic Rooster there. I was wearing a suit and I was mistaken for a record company executive. They wore suits in those days!"

In 1979 Fashion played The Mayfair Suite, supporting The Damned, who apparently were re-christened The Doomed for the occasion. Luke James explains:

"It was supposed to be a benefit to raise money for Sid Vicious' legal defence in New York City for the Nancy Spungeon murder trial. So... The Doomed."

A final off-the-wall memory (maybe it was a weird place after all!) comes from Tom Ward who, after enthusing about seeing Led Zeppelin and Black Sabbath there, mentions that "a pal of mine unknowingly drank all of Ozzy's cider." Sadly we have no information about Ozzy's reaction!

The Regan circuit

Back in the heyday of Brum Beat the Regan circuit of four venues was at the heart of Birmingham's live music scene and in the early 1970s they were still playing their part. There were two Plazas, in Handsworth and in Old Hill in the Black Country, The Ritz, a former cinema in Kings Heath, and an Irish club in Small Heath, the Garryowen, which they renamed for a time The Brum Kavern. The echo of the Liverpool club scene was not coincidental.

The Regans were Mary and Joe, known locally as Ma and Pa Regan, who came to Birmingham from Ireland as teenagers. The driving force was the formidable, slightly scary Ma who made the decisions about which bands were to play in her ballrooms. The Wolverhampton *Express & Star* cannily described her as "a softly spoken Irish ex-school teacher who uses the same psychology with the groups as she did with school pupils – discipline and organisation." The affable, genial Joe would run the show and greet the bands, somewhat incongruously, attired in black suit, white shirt and bowtie.

The venues are now places of legend where many folk got their first experience of the top acts of the day, not only the stars of the Brian Epstein empire such as The Beatles and Gerry and the Pacemakers, but The Rolling Stones, The Animals, The Kinks, Manfred Mann, Dusty Springfield and Pink Floyd as well as visiting Americans such as Jerry Lee Lewis, Del Shannon and Brenda Lee.

With four large venues, each operating nightly for five or six hours, the appetite for bands was enormous. The Regans would book a local band to play one-hour support sets on the same evening in two different venues several miles apart. Although the halls had their own in-house PA systems, the bands still had to hump their amplifiers, drumkit and keyboards into the band van, drive possibly from Handsworth to Old Hill, unload and set up at the next gig with no sound-check.

Unsurprisingly there was no shortage of bands lining up to appear on the Regan circuit. Although the standard fee was a princely £12 a performance, a good band could play six or more shows in a week and, as one band-member recalled:

"Coming round on that revolving stage at the Plaza Old Hill was a real event. You felt like a star."

A tale of the unexpected from Birmingham University

AUL McCARTNEY AND WINGS GIVE SURPRISE CONCERT TO 700 IN DEB. HALL

'ON THE ROAD' PAUL STRIKES BIRMINGHAM

by **PAUL TAYLOR**

PAUL McCARTNEY and his band Wings casually drove up to the Union at 5.15 p.m. on Monday and asked if they could play there that evening. After talking with Events Committee and looking over Deb. Hall, it was decided that the concert should go on. Word quickly got round that McCartney was going to play, and posters were hastily made. By seven o'clock a queue had started to form. By seven-thirty about

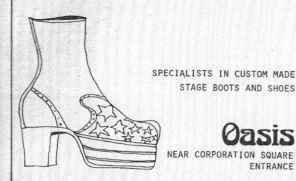

Chapter 5
Capital of rock'n'roll

Birmingham rock music entered the 1970s with a roar with Black Sabbath, but that roar hardly diminished through the decade with an astonishing series of bands, some of which made it to the top of the charts – others didn't, but deserved to. Funny that Birmingham's never seen as the rock'n'roll capital of the UK – all the evidence is there!

In 1978 one of the more controversial Birmingham bands burst upon the scene. They were the hugely successful Dexys Midnight Runners whose very name was rooted in controversy. It was inspired by Dexedrine, used as a recreational drug by the Northern Soul scene as it reputedly supplied the fuel to keep on dancing through till dawn.

The first single, *Dance Stance*, charted at Number 40 in

In 1978 one of the more controversial Birmingham bands burst upon the scene. They were the hugely successful Dexys Midnight Runners

---

1979, to be followed by a string of hits including *Geno* and *Come on, Eileen*, but seemingly the band was never a happy unit. A series of personnel changes left only the leader, Kevin Rowland, as an ever-present. As a response to the smart uniforms of other bands, Kevin togged out the Dexys in donkey jackets and woolly hats. He refused media interviews, preferring to communicate his thoughts to the public through advertisements and pronouncements in his soul boy drug vernacular. In response the *New Musical Express* wrote, "Dexys deliver emotional fascism and are a perversion of soul music, no tenderness, no sex, no laughter."

Perhaps many people's salient memory of the band is of them removing their master-tapes from Abbey Road Studios, high-tailing it back to Birmingham and reportedly holding EMI to ransom for an increased royalty rate. In retrospect, appropriate behaviour for the unforgettable soul rebels!

The band that John Peel repeatedly said was his favourite 1970s band was a quartet from Billesley. The three Jones brothers, Josh, Jack and Johnny, together with their childhood friend, Jim Doherty, were The Quads whose 1979 protest single, *There Must be Thousands,* charted at a relatively modest Number 66, but inspired the iconic broadcaster to write, "I have to say I would not swap my single of *There Must be Thousands* for the entire recorded works of Oasis and Radiohead."

Their later single, *Gotta Getta Job*, became an anthem for protest marches by the unemployed. The band even took to the road, joining the 1981 now-famous March for Jobs in Stoke-on-Trent where they played an evening show for the protesters before marching with them to London.

Somehow The Quads never achieved the lasting fame confidently predicted by those who know about these things. As they moved on, the band's publicity photographs in black suits with vicars' dog collars proved prophetic. Guitarist and singer Jack Jones now lives in New Zealand where he works – as a vicar.

In the early 1970s, in discos throughout the city, one Birmingham band was a guaranteed dance floor filler. This was Muscles. Inspired by the music of James Brown and the like, Muscles delivered a high-powered set of originals and standards. Although they were regulars at niteries across the city, Eddie Fewtrell's Rebecca's was their regular stomping ground, with crowds lining up to get in long before the time Muscles were due to hit.

They released a series of singles on Birmingham record label, Big Bear, all of which became regional dance floor hits, supported by club DJs and local radio, and released across

Top Birmingham band The Move looking suitably soulful

Garbo rising from the grave promoting his single, *Only Death is Fatal/Won't You Come to My Funeral?*

Birmingham rock band, Hannibal

Photos by Jim Simpson

Not a synod of vicars, but The Quads

Radio Plays for week ending Friday December 5th 1975.

MUSCLES.

Rosko	Sat 29th November.
Tony Blackburn	Mon 1st December.
Tony Blackburn	Thurs 4th December.
Johnny Walker	Frid 5th December.
D.L.T.	Mon 1st December.
D.L.T.	Thurs 4th December.
Paul Burnett	Sun 30th November.
Paul Burnett	Sun 7th December.

N.B. Noel Edmunds show not available.

Radio Luxembourg . . . . Playlisted.

BOB PEGG

Open House . . . . Tues 2nd December.

HUMPHREY LYTTLETON.

Jazz Club . . . . Sun 30th November.

LEE KONITZ

Jazz Club . . . . Sun 30th November.

Europe. The band suddenly found themselves touring Europe, opening the shows for such name bands as The Commodores, The Fatback Band, The Ohio Players, Gloria Gaynor, KC and the Sunshine Band, Tower of Power and Kool and the Gang – they were even the UK/European rhythm section for the outrageous Disco Tex and the Sexolettes!

Singer, guitarist and keyboard player, Geoff Brown, delighted in telling swooning girl fans that he came from California – which he did in a way – not the California of West Coast America, but the outlying Birmingham suburb of the same name!

Unsurprisingly, with so many American bluesmen making Birmingham their second home during the 1970s, some unlikely musical partnerships were struck up, invariably involving Muscles and Big Bear Records. Much taken with the extrovert and entertaining performances of Cousin Joe from New Orleans, Geoff Brown wrote the songs, *You're Never Too Old to Boogie* – Joe was, after all, **67** years old at the time – and *I'm Cousin Joe from New Orleans* which were recorded by Cousin Joe, with Muscles' backing. Geoff also penned, and Muscles backed, the single, *Boogie Down wit' The Boogie Man*, by Gene "The Mighty Flea" Connors, from Birmingham, Alabama.

Muscles also had the distinction of playing on *Okavanga Swamp*, the only recorded vocal by Simple Minds drummer Mel Gaynor. Mel had re-located to Birmingham to join the band and for his vocal debut (and, apparently, swansong) on record Muscles, for some mysterious reason, went under the name Zulu.

When Muscles had run their course, Geoff Brown, always a technical whiz, set up a company making and selling computer games, fast became a millionaire and moved to Santa Monica, eventually fulfilling his early claim to be from California.

Above: Birmingham band Muscles on the radio – and Humphrey Lyttelton (yet again!) mis-spelt

A fine display of Muscles!

...land SOUNDS — Paul Cole looks at one of the Midlands biggest success stories

ELO

The Electric Light Orchestra, you might say, all started off with semolina pilchards climbing up the Eiffel Tower.

Rock mastermind Roy Wood was greatly impressed by the Beatles' orchestral outings on tracks like "I Am The Walrus" and "Strawberry Fields Forever."

And being Roy Wood, he just had to take the idea a little further. A crazy dream was born — the perfect fusion of orchestra and rock band in one perfect working unit.

Jeff Lynne, hearing of the project, quit his legendary Idle Race and joined Roy and Bev Bevan in the last line-up of the marvellous Move — Birmingham's major contribution to rock'n'roll.

ELO was originally planned as a parallel project to the Move, and while the whole show was being put on the road, Move singles continued to flow — "Brontosaurus," "When Alice Comes Back to the Farm," "Chinatown," "Tonight" and "California Man."

Rock fans had the distinctly baffling sensation of deja vu, seeing first The Move and then ELO appearing on television.

It was in 1971 that ELO first emerged on record. The embryonic Electric Light Orchestra, bearded, shaded and mysterious, cut an experimental album of the same name — and produced on the way their first hit, "10538 Overture."

At this time the line-up was Roy Wood, Jeff Lynne, Bev Bevan, Rick Price, Hugh McDowell and any friends who happened to be around, like Richard Tandy.

Then, almost immediately in 1972, visionary Roy Wood quit, claiming that too much attention was being lavished on himself instead of the band as a whole.

Difficulties in getting ELO to work well live, and the frustration of the first chaotic — and catastrophic — performances did little for the Dream.

Roy formed the whacky Wizzard

— a good time rock'n'roll band who produced classic singles — and took Rick and Hugh with him.

Jeff Lynne took a look at what was left, and with Bev Bevan, recruited himself an orchestra featuring musicians with classical or rock training, but rarely both. "ELO II", issued in February 1973 was more controlled and featured the band's showstopper — an orchestrated version of Chuck Berry's "Roll Over Beethoven."

By the time the third album "On The Third Day" was released later that year, Hugh had returned from Wizzard and young Mik Kaminski had joined up — forming the basis of ELO as they are today.

"Showdown" — with its soul overtones, the best single yet — was culled from the album, and the superb "Eldorado" followed in 1974.

Bassist Michael De Albuquerque and cellist Mike Edwards left before the fifth album "Face The Music", and the line-up for ELO's

...cond gold album was [illegible] Jeff, Bev, Hugh, Mik, [illegible] Groucutt, Melvyn Gale and [illegible]

Hit singles like "Ma-Ma Belle" and "Evil Woman" follow with the sixth album "A New World Record" cheered the [illegible] with songs like "Telephone [illegible]

ELO was now an independent high quality rock pop band, the realisation of Roy Wood's d[illegible] — and the 1977 double set "Out Of The Blue" was the band's finest hour.

Now established as a major force in rock music, ELO [illegible]loped a sound all of their own, became the best singles [illegible] since The Beatles.

The latest album "Disco[illegible] goes even further as Jeff [illegible] strives for new ideas with [illegible] Diary Of Horace Wimp", on[illegible] the best pop singles ever re[illegible]

Gone is the chaos of the [illegible] days, and gone are the ov[illegible] ambitious orchestral backd[illegible] ELO remain ELO — a truly [illegible]ginal talent.

Mik's holiday for strings

When violinist Mik Kamin[illegible] burst forth with his own ban[illegible] Violinski, E.L.O. fans took a dee[illegible] breath.

And when he wasn't even credited [illegible] E.L.O.'s smash "Discovery" album, [illegible] worried fans took on frowns deeper tha[illegible] those of sad Horace Wimp.

Things looked ominous. Was Mik playing second fiddle to Jeff Lynne's ass[illegible] orchestral guests?

The answer was short and sweet — [illegible] Violinski album entitled "No Cause F[illegible] Alarm", an official statement on th[illegible] record.

In fact Mik's solo excursion is just th[illegible] first of many by the members of th[illegible] Electric Light Orchestra.

Explains Mik: "All of us have bee[illegible] working on projects of our own, and ther[illegible] should be a lot of solo material comin[illegible] out in the future.

Yet another chart-topping Birmingham band, the Electric Light Orchestra

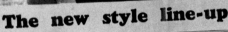

The new style line-up

THE NEW TEAM... the Electric Light Orchestra players (above) and fans in a special line-up.

Left to right, back row: Jeff Lynne, Ray Martin, Bev Bevan. Front: George Smith, Richard Tandy and Geoff Commander.

Jeff, Bev and Roy Wood (of the Move, and formerly with ELO and now leading Wizzard) are all Birmingham City fans, and have been for years, so what is more natural than getting Blues' men Ray Martin and George Smith along to join in?

The leaders

ELO are an extension of the Move, as are Wizzard, and thereby lies a complicated story that Dennis Detheridge tackles inside.

It is sufficient to say that Jeff Lynne and Bev Bevan are the leaders of the band (ELO that is).

The single taken from their first ELO album — 10538 Overture — is doing big business in the charts.

● For more of the story turn inside ▶

TUESDAY is in the 'MAIL'

Circling round the top

MEN APART: Bev Bevan and Jeff Lynne, who guide E.L.O. and Roy Wood, who split to find a Wizzard.

DENNIS DETHERIDGE SAYS...

E.L.O.

NO one is more surprised at the success of 10538 Overture by The Electric Light Orchestra than Jeff Lynne, composer of the number and the band's leading light since the departure of Roy Wood.

"It's a track off the E.L.O. album and we only released it as a single as a way of getting people to know what we were like," admitted the 24-year-old guitarist.

"It was nothing more than a trailer for the album really.

"But getting into the charts has helped us a lot. For a start, it means we can support ourselves, without having to rely on money from The Move to help us along.

"And it has given us an opportunity to play for big audiences. We have been getting a tremendous reception all over the country and bookings are coming in thick and fast."

BROKEN DREAM

But what about Roy Wood, the guy who walked out of a musical dream when he quit the E.L.O.?

Does he have any regrets now that 10538 Overture is doing well in the charts?

"None at all," he said emphatically. "I'm very involved with my new band, Wizzard.

"Naturally, we need a hit if we are to pull big crowds, but I'm in no hurry to get a single out by Wizzard.

"I prefer to wait until we have something strong enough to make the charts."

Although Roy virtually handed over the E.L.O. on a plate to Jeff Lynne and drummer Bev Bevan, the three musicians will continue to record together as The Move, so we can look forward to a follow-up to California Man.

Roy, writer of all the Move's hits, rejects any suggestion that he might be tempted to keep his best material for Wizzard, whose line-up includes former Move man Rick Price on bass.

DIFFERENT SENSE

"A song that suits The Move won't necessarily be any good for my new band," he explained.

"Wizzard are playing rock'n roll but not in the same sense as The Move. It's rock'n roll with a difference."

Clearly, apart from contractual obligations, it is in the interests of Roy, Jeff and Bev to keep The Move together. They have done very nicely, thank you, out of the group's hit parade consistency.

Wood has a £42,000 mansion on the Worcestershire-Staffordshire border; Lynne has just moved into a country residence with 10 acres of land in Worcestershire; and Bev

is building up a chain of "Heavyhead" record shops.

The four-car garage at Roy's home is used for Wizzard rehearsals whilst the E.L.O. have been busy working on new arrangements at the Old Moseleians Rugby Club in Lugtrout Lane, Solihull.

Jeff and Bev are personal friends of the Birmingham City football team — although Bev is a Wolves fan and treks to St. Andrew's only on alternate weeks — and Blues players call in on their way from the nearby Damson Lane training ground.

The popularity of 10538 Overture is earning Jeff Lynne belated recognition as a songwriter.

What he is not generally realised that his recorded material includes two LP's and five singles with The Idle Race, three Move "B" sides, songs on The Move's Looking On and Message From The Country albums and five compositions on the E.L.O. LP.

What effect has the loss of Roy Wood had on the E.L.O.?

"We are giving more thought to the arrangements," said Jeff. "We have more exciting ideas and different variations on themes.

"There is also more freedom in the arrangements. A lot of the songs we were doing with the E.L.O. were strict without much room for improvisation. Now there's scope for these free passages.

"Our Mellotron synthesiser is also helping us to introduce new sounds. 10538 Overture is just the start of what's to come from the E.L.O."

Coming shortly...

BIRMINGHAM - born Carl Wayne, former lead singer with The Move but now seeking solo success, will be getting heavy TV exposure soon.

Apart from making a re-appearance in the Crossroads serial, he is also lined up for a

No

Crown (and other) punks

The Crown on Hill Street keeps bursting into this narrative from all sorts of angles, being a centre for one sort of popular music after another. In the late 1970s it was the punk scene that took over and the Crown punks became an identifiable group with a political and social impact, no less than a musical one.

Round about 1976 Tom Pickering, landlord of The Crown in the glory days of Henry's Blueshouse, returned to the pub which had become run down and troubled by anti-social behaviour. Barman Billy Dupre, a hippie in an earlier decade, got Tom's permission for a punk-friendly music policy. For two or three years the punks dominated the scene until around 1979 skinheads with Far Right politics began to make their presence felt. However, Tom seems to have successfully brokered peace between the various tribes: there was even no real friction between the mixed race ska/two tone fans and the Far Right.

Among bands popular with the Crown Punks were GBH and Drongos for Europe. Elsewhere Matthew Edwards recalls seeing TV Eye ("along with The Prefects Birmingham's best punk band") at the Rainbow Suite and there were also punk all-dayers at Barbarella's. Martin Booth's splendid collection of photographs documents punks at Barbarella's brilliantly.

The Prefects, Birmingham's first punk band, had a suitably controversial career. Formed after brothers Alan and Paul Apperley advertised in the *Birmingham Evening Mail* for a singer (Robert Lloyd got the gig, a certain Frank Skinner missed out), they played their first gig at a private party which ended

in a police raid. Start as you mean to go on – their first gig at a public venue, Rebecca's, ended when they were driven off-stage by bottles thrown at them in response to the song *Birmingham's a Shithole*. Still John Peel liked them – and they recorded two John Peel Sessions.

For the second of these sessions The Prefects borrowed two members of the garage punk band TV Eye. Originally formed by five teenagers at Moseley Art School, the band was comparatively short-lived, but had a minor return to fame in 2017 when their 1977 recordings were finally released!

In 1978 the Birmingham punk band Bullets had their day in the sun – or, rather, their day in the sights of the mighty *Sun* newspaper. The band's single, *Girl on Page 3*, dealt with the woes of a pin-up, centre of attention today, fish and chip wrapping (or worse) tomorrow. The record company, somewhat naively – or should that be mischievously? – approached the media giant to suggest a joint promotion of the disc. The response came in the form of a solicitor's letter threatening litigation, injunctions and claims for damages appropriate to infringing the copyright of the *Sun* which owned the rights to the words "Page Three".

Risking the wrath of the Murdoch empire, the record company proceeded to release *Girl on Page 3*, backed by *Grammar School Girls*, with the production jokily credited to Jim Slip. And the illustration on the record sleeve showed what's worse than fish and chip wrapping: a close-up illustration of a primitive lavatory, with toilet roll replaced by torn copies of...but you've guessed which page of which newspaper!

...Not forgotten

Cissy Stone was a star in many people's eyes. Glamorous but cute, she had a terrific on-stage personality – and, most importantly, the girl could really sing. When she recorded for Decca Records in 1976, her debut single, *Gone But Not Forgotten*, was a dead cert for the charts. It was enthusiastically received, received heavy airplay, but, for whatever reason, didn't quite chart, although it did take her to places that normal mortals can only dream of – having Marvin Gaye play piano in her band, for instance.

In 1978, to the surprise of many, Cissy joined the French electronic soul band, Didier Marouani and Space, replacing Madeline Bell. Her space disco fad didn't last long and she was soon back in the UK singing great soul music which she does to this day. *Gone but Not Forgotten* remains a northern soul classic, but there's one piece of Cissy's 1970s action that has yet to see the light of day. Muscles' Geoff Brown wrote a song for her, *If It Relaxes Your Mind*, which she recorded, backed by Muscles. Everybody believed it to be hit material, but intriguingly it was never released. The reason? Apparently it was considered "too steamy"! Maybe, one day...

sounds

Bullets
Birmingham

FIRST TIME I saw Bullets I was mightily impressed by the way they hung together on a stage little bigger than a kitchen table. And seeing them at Barbarellas where they've got room to breathe the effect, as they say in some advert or other, is shattering.

They've tightened up considerably and if they could still gel a little more that's only a minor criticism.

They open up with a hammering 'You'll Never Get Out Of This World Alive' and the pace rarely flags from that point on. Old favourite 'Overnight Sensation' bites at your heels as soon as the last chords of 'World' are fading into the heady atmosphere. It always was a good number, now with Chris Stanley's bass pumping away and Harry's assured lead blazing away it's become a great song. Other old favourites still make up most of the set. 'Scream Machine' and the jazz-cool 'Dinosaur', on which Steve Thomas takes over for vocals, pull the applause but for me the high spots come on the new numbers, especially 'So What'. Basic simple three chords, aggressive guitar (and special mention here for John Shaw) sterling driving drum (Graham Spears) and scruff of the neck bass; Harry coming through like a power-punch as he snaps out the lyrics 'So what, I never wrote a song about you. So what, you never wrote a song about me'. Looking back at the song in the clear light of morning I still think it's in the same instant-commercial-but-with-a-layer-of-class bracket as Free's 'All Right Now', and we all know what happened to that.

I'm not just being smart ass when I say that Bullets are shooting stars, maybe it's a bad pun, but it sure as hell is a good band. — MIKE DAVIES.

bULLETS

NOW AVAILABLE ON RECORD!

girl on page 3

grammar school girls

Big Bear Records
190 Monument Road
Birmingham
England
021-454-7020

BB1

The New Musical Express on a musical scandal!

Photos by Martin Booth

In March 1972 King Kong came to town in the form of the 18 foot fibre glass statue that landed in the Bull Ring's Manzoni Gardens and straight into the affections of many ordinary Brummies, such as young Norm Elliott:

"Mom took me to see him the day after he was put into Manzoni Gardens and it was magical for a little kid."

For some reason those in power didn't share the public's affection for King Kong and soon he was as neglected and ignored as only a 140-stone gorilla can be. After being briefly exhibited in Gosta Green, Kong's next venture was to front a second-hand car dealership on the Stratford Road where his neighbour was the former Holy Trinity Church. At Christmas he suffered the indignity of being dressed as Santa Claus which was nothing to the embarrassment he felt when painted in tartan – and later, even worse, in pink – when he was sited in Edinburgh. King Kong's long and winding journey, often unwanted and unloved, now has him in a garden in Cumbria, waiting for fame to knock again.

And – amazingly! – 2021 saw the release of the film *King Rocker* about King Kong and Robert Lloyd, frontman of 1970s group The Nightingales, once memorably described as "the misfits' misfit". When you've been painted pink in Edinburgh, it must be rather nice to feature in "an anti-rockumentary which weaves the story of Birmingham's undervalued underdog autodidact with that of the city's forgotten public sculpture of King Kong."

Eating out

Hungry at the end of the night and no all-night café in view? Not to worry, the tea wagons and pie stalls of the night economy stepped into the beach. Fran Hawkes remembers "waiting for a nightservice bus in Colmore Row with a baked potato from the guy in pigeon park" while Chris Pitt favoured a hot dog or hamburger from the stand in Victoria Square before catching the last bus. Rather grumpily Paul Harris dismisses such extravagances in favour of walking home with a bag of chips, while Jim Cronin introduces a gourmet touch:

"The tea wagon opposite the Kardomah was the in-place once Le Metro kicked out. Steak and kidney pie and Bovril was the dish of choice."

News of Birmingham's favourite gorilla

King Kong comes to Brum

THE only true beauty of the film world has finally found a resting-place in Birmingham, the Florence of the Midlands. Just in case you haven't been along to admire/deface this monument to the good taste of Birmingham City Corporation, IT proudly stands, about twenty feet high, slap-bang in the cultural centre of the city, i.e., the Bull Ring.

King Kong, his red eyes aglow and his smooth plastic fur glistening gently in its rain-drenched surroundings, chokes silently on the cataclysmic effects of carbon monoxide, cigarette smoke, industrial effluent and the odd molecule of air. His head was proudly held but for a few moments and then fell dolefully on to the crowds of connoisseurs sipping their Brew XI in admiration.

There is but one flaw in this majestic masterpiece and that is the task of visible means of ascertaining whether Kong is in indeed a King. The inalienable truth is that IT is King Kastrate. This, we believe, is due to the intervention of a notable female city councillor who, unable to block the King's erection, insisted on his castration.

However, the sad episode of the Pièta in Rome looms heavily over Kong's aesthetic majesty. Four guardsmen will be posted around Kong in dreary vigil, whilst the City Fathers decide a means of enclosing him in glass. Knowing the learned gentlemen's haste, those guardsmen are likely to be pensioned off, their only claim to glory that of having guarded a King Boob.

Pie stall with bikers behind The Crown

Photo by Martin Booth

DiRTY
STOP OUTS
GUIDE

Photos by Martin Booth

THE BARREL ORGAN

FORTHCOMING ATTRACTIONS

NDAY   THE ANDROIDS
SDAY   THE ANDROIDS
RSDAY   LITTLE WILLY
DAY'S
RDAY

THE BARREL OR

Top local bands line up at the Barrel Organ Photo by Jim Simpson

DiRTY STOP OUTS GUIDE

Photos by Martin Booth

Chapter 6
Folk, reggae and soul

The Ian Campbell Folk Group in action
Photo by Jim Simpson

In the 1970s Birmingham was a seething cauldron of musical activity. At the time the *New Musical Express* estimated that there were 500 bands in the city. And not all of them by any means fell into the familiar rock/beat/pop mould.

For instance, the Jug o' Punch Folk Club was based every Thursday in the Digbeth Civic Hall back room. With a capacity of 500 and usually absolutely packed, it was the largest and most important folk club in the UK and possibly in Europe. It was organised by Ian Campbell who, at the age of 17, had moved from Aberdeen with his father David.

Having started out as the Clarion Skiffle Group in 1956, Ian Campbell Folk Group had already established themselves

as pioneers of the developing folk scene in the 1960s. By 1970 star fiddle player Dave Swarbrick had moved on, but the group still included Ian's sister, Lorna, and bass guitarist Dave Pegg, formerly of the Uglys and Locomotive. Eventually Pegg, too, moved on, to join with Swarbrick in Fairport Convention, pioneers of folk-rock, yet another music genre to originate in Birmingham (sort of!).

By all accounts the Campbell Folk Group were pretty eager to play in most places at most times:

"They used to hang out in pubs quite a lot in Moseley and Kings Heath. There was one pub in Kings Heath that used to open about 10.00 am on Sundays and a few of them would be playing there, too." (Robin Westley Martin)

Laurel Aitken, the Godfather of Ska, at Big Bear Records
Photo by Jim Simpson

Ian Campbell and the Birmingham skyline
Photo by Jim Simpson

"When I was at school at Saltley Grammar my English teacher arranged for them to come and play to our class. I think she used to frequent the Jug o' Punch. They were brilliant!" (David Burt)

Ian Campbell had four sons, three of whom, Ali, Robin and Duncan, went on to sing with reggae superstars, UB40.

Ian Campbell had four sons, three of whom, Ali, Robin and Duncan, went on to sing with reggae superstars, UB40

Only David continued the folk music tradition, though with a distinctly political edge.

Birmingham's music scene, even then, had a distinctly cosmopolitan flavour. The city's West Indian immigrants brought with them calypso, rock steady and ska. By the 1970s a stroll down Soho Road or through Lozells would be accompanied by great island sounds coming from houses, pubs and clubs. Over in Balsall Heath bhangra was born out of a fusion of Punjabi and Western music.

The West Indian blues parties and shebeens in Handsworth were at the heart of it, the Birmingham equivalent of all-night tea parties in the Caribbean. Typically unlicensed, held in empty houses, these community events would see visitors paying an entrance fee, electricity wired to street lights and music over mobile sound speakers, competing with each other to deliver the heaviest bass. Stripped down to drum and bass, with plenty of echo and reverb, the result was referred to as "riddim" and the chat, rap and chants of DJs were known as "toasting".

The parties would attract audiences from as far afield as London, Manchester and Bristol. The Caribbean community was close knit, but welcomed large numbers of white ska fans.

As sociologist Dick Hebdige wrote, "This is one of the few places left in Britain where it is still possible for a white man to get into a shebeen without wearing a blue uniform and kicking the door down."

Veteran radio presenter Chicken George has memories of the West Indian community in the 1970s. Having lost his sight as a boy, he competed in the 1972 Disabled Olympics at 60 and 100 metres, taking a silver and a bronze before upping that to two silvers in 1976. George came to Birmingham in the late 1970s, recalling such important Caribbean clubs as the Monte Carlo and the Ridgeway, as well as the original Handsworth restaurant run by Rustie Lee (later a noted television personality) next to her mother's bakery.

Ruby Turner and Cousin Joe with Ray King, famed for his West Bromwich Albion anthem
Photo by Jim Simpson

The Continental Club, sited just opposite the Monte Carlo in Soho Road, was notable on two counts. It was a cellar club and it stayed open until six in the morning. Nearby Soho Hill was home to several West Indian clubs, among them the FCF Club – that's Faith and Confidence Finance – not the most enticing name for what was, in fact, a pretty cool club. FCF opened in 1971 as a members only club. While annual membership cost only £2, nomination by two existing members was required in order to be accepted – so they didn't welcome just any Tom, Dick or Rudi!

As for Chicken George himself, having long been a stalwart of PCRL (People's Community Radio Link), founded to heal tensions after the 1985 Handsworth riots, he eventually founded New Style Radio, the first legal black radio station in Birmingham.

Towards the end of the 1970s the Caribbean influence led to a clutch of great new Birmingham bands, spearheaded by three reggae bands who were each destined to dent charts worldwide in the early 1980s.

Frederick Waite Senior had enjoyed significant chart success with Jamaican rock steady combo The Techniques before immigrating to the UK and settling in Birmingham. In 1979 he re-emerged briefly as co-lead singer, along with his son, also Frederick – known as Junior – of a new band. This was the extremely youthful and undeniably musical Handsworth reggae band Musical Youth. Junior and fellow-band members Kelvin and Michael Grant were all still at school, so, unsurprisingly feeling out of place, Frederick Senior quickly stood down. Still schoolboys, Musical Youth were soon featuring at pubs and clubs across the city, taking the first steps to international stardom which came with their still infectious hit, *Pass the Dutchie*, in 1982.

Meanwhile, across the city, in the hitherto hippie suburb of Moseley, eight young unemployed men whose parentage included English, Welsh, Irish, Jamaican, Scots and Yemeni decided to take up instruments and form a band to play the music they loved – reggae. Their name was a no-brainer, it had to reflect their work – or lack of it – status.

The unemployment benefit document was known as UB 40 and that was their choice. The title of their first album, released in 1980, was *Signing Off*, referring to their signing off from the dole – a nice, down to earth, very Brummie touch.

UB40's fans shared the group's social conscience. Tim Jennings, then a student in the city, remembers an early concert at Digbeth Civic Hall in the days when such contrasting

movements as Rock Against Racism and The National Front had a strong appeal to the young:

"At that time it was known that Pollyanna's was operating a racist admissions policy, so after the concert what seemed like half the audience set out to march from Digbeth to protest at the club in Newhall Street. When we got there it all fizzled out, but the march itself was pretty dramatic. The marchers were carrying torches and for about 100 of us there were what seemed to be 200 police, fending off skinheads from The National Front who were trying to get at us."

Musicians were instantly impressed with UB 40. Take Gillon Jacoby, for instance:

"I was at UB 40's first gig at the Hare and Hounds in Kings Heath. The band I was in, Fast Relief, played with them a few times. They were a class act from the very beginning. It's no surprise they did so well. We also supported Musical Youth on their first tour when the father of two of them, Freddie Waite, was still in the band."

The most uncompromisingly political of the UK's reggae bands was Steel Pulse, formed in 1975 by five kids from Handsworth Boys' School

---

Or Paul Harris:

"My first band, the Dum Dum Boys, supported UB 40 on an anti-racism gig. That was 1979 and UB 40 hadn't yet released a record. Ranking Roger (RIP) was our drummer. My third band supported UB 40 on their first tour of the UK. Musical Youth were also on the tour and we all played the Odeon."

The most uncompromisingly political of the UK's reggae bands was Steel Pulse, formed in 1975 by five kids from Handsworth Boys' School who went on to become the first non-Jamaican band ever to win a Grammy Award for Best Reggae Band. Always a roots reggae combo, they were first inspired by Bob Marley and the Wailers, but were deemed unsuited to appear at local Caribbean venues because of their Rastafarian beliefs. Interestingly they found their niche in punk venues, became deeply involved in the Rock Against Racism movement and toured with leading punk bands such as The Stranglers. The band's first single was a savage indictment of racism, *Ku Klux Klan*, and their ground-breaking album, *Handsworth Revolution*, in 1978 now seems ominously titled in view of events in the 1980s.

In the mid-1970s Superbad, almost a Sylvester family band with Charlie, Willis and Steve, ruled the Disco Soul roost along with Muscles, the bosses of blue-eyed soul, and Stax Explosion, featuring the now legendary soul survivor Roy Gee Hemmings. Soon their fame spread as far south as the London office of Magnet Records and the ever-open ears of top producer Pete Waterman.

Pete quickly picked up on the undeniable talent of Roy Gee, decided that all he needed was the right band to take him to the top of the dance-floor charts, and set about band-building. Having decided on the singer, front man and songwriter, he came up with a name – the J.A.L.N. Band

– and recruited the rest of the guys: saxophonists Tex Flint and Willis Sylvester, brothers Charlie on guitar and Steve on bass, Sam Fortune on keyboards and 18-year-old drummer Ronnie Johns.

As the hits came, The J.A.L.N. Band – for anybody who doesn't remember, that's Just Another Lonely Night – seemed to be around every street corner, touring incessantly, there every time a radio was switched on and

> ### Maybe the guys in the band had differing ideas about the direction they should take, but after three years Roy walked and the band split

seemingly on *Top of the Pops* every second week. Maybe the guys in the band had differing ideas about the direction they should take, but after three years Roy walked and the band split, leaving memories of that superflash stage performance and those monster flares.

Roy Gee Hemmings remembers that his first impulse was to re-form Stax Explosion, but by now it was the 1980s and he was persuaded that by this time it was not a good idea to have the word "explosion" in a band's name. So he decided to proceed as Roy Gee and Energee, cutting a well reviewed 12-inch single, but no longer making a dent in the charts.

Roy was then surprised – most pleasantly – at the next opportunity that came knocking at his door in the form of

George Treadwell, manager of the legendary New York vocal giants, The Drifters. To Roy it was a no-brainer: he upped sticks and moved to New York to create history with his 16-year tenure, making him the longest-serving Drifter ever. Now, back in Birmingham where it all started, he fronts his showband, The Dictionary of Soul.

Birmingham: Musical melting pot

Here's an interesting musical encounter: the 16-year-old Francella Ruby Turner, born in Montego Bay, Jamaica, and 67-year-old Pleasant Joseph, born in Wallace, Louisiana. Ruby Turner had lived in Handsworth since the age of nine and was right at the beginning of a long and illustrious career as a hitmaking soul singer and actress. Professionally known as Cousin Joe from New Orleans, sometimes known as Brother Joshua when recording gospel songs, Pleasant Joseph was touring Europe in support of his album *Gospel Wailing, Jazz Playing, Soul Shouting, Tap Dancing Bluesman from New Orleans*. They met in the Edgbaston HQ of Big Bear Records and found they had a lot of music to talk about for a couple of hours. Had they hung around for another hour or so, they would have met the Godfather of Ska who had dropped in for a coffee and a chat. Lorenzo, better known as Laurel, Aitken, from Santiago de Cuba, was living in Leicester and must have spent much of his life in the recording studio as he recorded a total of 120 singles as well as a bunch of great albums.

Like they say, sit down long enough in Birmingham and the whole world of music will come to you!

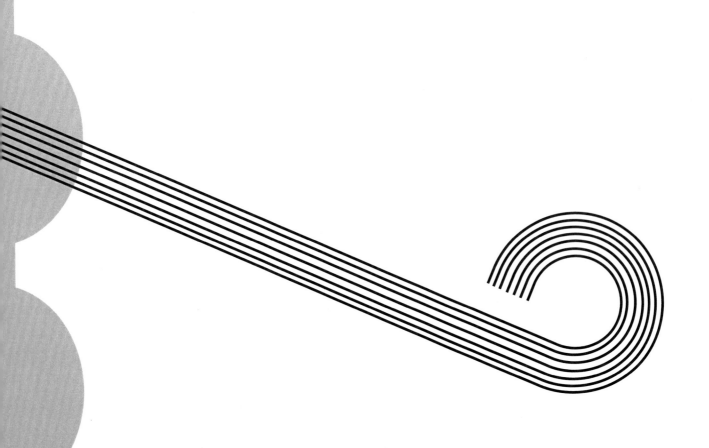

Chapter 7
Life in the hippie village

"**B**ack in the day," said Pete The Feet, "you could do what you wanted, so I took my shoes off – and I couldn't be bothered to put them back on. So I'm not going to do it now, just so I can get into a pub."

Since the 1960s Moseley has been recognised as the hippie village of Birmingham. Just four miles from the centre of the city, it has become known for the unconventional life-style of many of its inhabitants, more than a passing interest in certain herbs, off the wall music and arts, and its characters.

Foremost among those is probably Pete The Feet, a native of Cumbria who, having moved to Moseley and married his ever-loving wife Jenny, decided that he would never again wear shoes. He remained barefoot for half a century, claiming that shoes gave him sweaty feet and made him nervous and therefore angry.

Formerly a telephone exchange engineer, William Peter McKenzie became a much loved figure in the village. He became the object of yet more interest when folk spotted that he had both his little fingers missing, amputated as a result of carpal tunnel syndrome. Pete had retained the missing fingers, embalmed, and he carried one in his pocket, always willing to show it and hand it over for examination to a startled acquaintance. The other, by the way, adorned his mantelpiece at home.

Following a heart attack he converted his mobility scooter, registration PTF 1, to look like a Harley Davidson. His illness didn't seem to have dimmed his enthusiasm for life. He still cheerily distributed his handmade leather cigarette lighter holders, bearing his own twin-foot logo, still wore his Stetson

Since the 1960s Moseley has been recognised as the hippie village of Birmingham. Just four miles from the centre of the city, it has become known for the unconventional life-style

hat and drank ale from the ever so slightly oversized pint glass he kept at his local – where he was always welcome, barefoot or not.

Pete Chatfield of Tea and Symphony knew Pete very well:

"George, the Tea and Symphony roadie, and I had been living in Moseley for a while and used to drink in the pubs. Some dudes in the Bulls Head decided we were 'undercover cops', so Pete came over and drank with us to dispel that theory. He made friends with us and came back to our flat one night to smoke some dope and eat jam sandwiches. He never left – moved in. Then he met Jenny. She moved into our top floor flat in 68 Trafalgar Road, so me and George moved out and up to 106 Trafalgar Road.

"George and I had met over in Yardley when I was in a rock band. George used to come and watch us rehearsing. We became good friends and, when I moved to Moseley, George came shortly after. We lived in one of the big three-storey houses split into bedsits on Church Road, number 40, top floor flat.

"That's where we first encountered Locomotive. It was winter, loads of snow on the ground, and they came down Forest Road towards Church Road and got stuck at the junction in their large grey Commer van. George and I went

Tea and Symphony smiling sweetly for the camera
Photo by Jim Simpson

ARTS LAB PARTY

MUSIC FROM:
THE
STEVE GIBBONS BAND
FROG
MICK GOLDING'S BAND

LIGHTSHOWS FROM:
ALFRED'S RAINBOW
CHROMATIC ORGASM

PLUS
DISCO
MOVIES
FOOD + DRINKS
....

TICKETS: 25p TO
MEMBERS + FRIENDS
FROM: THE ARTS LAB
TOWER ST., B'HAM B19 3UY
TEL: 021·359·4192

SAT. MAY 19. 9PM

and helped to push them on their way – they were going to a gig.

"Moseley at that time was full of student teachers, nurses, musos, hippies, doctors, a great place to walk safe at night – there was no major money in drugs, so no violence. Drinking frequently in the Bulls Head, the Fighting Cocks or Trafalgar, most of us knew the guys from the Drug Squad by sight. Their motto was, 'We don't mind you smoking it, but, if we catch you selling, you'll get busted.' Happy daze!

"After the pub most of the young folk in Moseley used to meet up in the Gigi Coffee Bar. It was run by Mrs. B who lived in the flats up Wake Green Road. One of the most popular waitresses was Lily Breedon whom I dated for some time. Each night when the Gigi closed Mrs. B would ask Lily and me if we would walk her home because she'd got the day's takings in her bag.

"Then there was the fish and chip shop by the traffic lights, run by Bernie who was married to a lovely Cypriot lady. It was the best chippie around and Bernie thought nothing of helping people out if they were down on their luck. I was in the chip shop one night after the pubs closed when Bernie suddenly vaulted the counter, ran across the road to the Bulls Head, knocked a guy out who was beating someone up, then calmly came back and asked, 'Right, who's next?'

"Besides Pete the Feet two characters left an enormous impression on me. Steve Lewis was a lovely gentle guy who

had great difficulty keeping away from the drugs or having control over them. Many times I walked him back to his place at the bottom of Church Road, but after several years of battling he succumbed to the drugs and died. Another was a lovely young lady whose name escapes me, but she obviously had some mental issues because she would often be seen naked on the streets of Moseley. Most of us knew her quite well and looked after her by covering her modesty and getting her safely home."

In an article for *The Guardian* in 2019 Kit de Waal sums up her life in Moseley in the 1960s and 1970s. A recent DNA test had revealed that her ancestry was as mixed as you might expect from a Moseley-ite of that period: more Irish than anything else, ancestors from Benin and Mali, thence to the Caribbean, and even a smattering of English. Incidental insights in the article sum up the "otherness" of Moseley: the handlebar-moustachioed art teacher in cord loons and a Ban the Bomb pendant with a wife with green hair or her claim that, at the age of 16, "if you weren't in a band, you were an oddity."

Of course some of the bands were oddities, too. Tea and Symphony provided the soundtrack to 1970s Moseley. They were eccentric, wildly unconventional and totally original. They had their own bizarre take on folk music, with meaningful lyrics and nice tunes, and were probably the first band to carry their own light show that invariably went

---

A FUNNY THING HAPPENED IN MOSELEY . . .

THE tall, thin young man with a European's apology for an Afro hairstyle asks us to wait for five minutes while he fixes the lighting in the small room above the Fighting Cocks pub in Moseley.

So we go downstairs for a drink and the next time we go up the young man helps people find stools and generally tries to make them happy in this small room in which air is quickly replaced by cigarette smoke.

Then he sits in front of us, this time the audience, and he is the man whose face is on the posters — Mr. John Dowie the man we have come to see.

The next morning while I am trying to recite his act to all and sundry I am asked to write this piece and with the post-show help of Mr. John Dowie here is the memory of a very funny evening.

☆ Laughter

I imagine the danger of writing about his show, "The Fifth Tango In Moseley," is that he will parody you in his act.

I don't want to be laughed at quite that much.

The judgment on any funny man must be how much laughter be creates.

If that seems obvious just

PETER JOHN laughs at Mr. JOHN DOWIE

think how many times you've laughed because the material is clever, or the props intricate, or the slapstick wild and looney.

And think how many times you've guffawed, laughed from the belly — Mr. John Dowie creased me.

If I may continue to be subjective I would like to explain that sometimes my wife is embarrassed when I start laughing.

This in understandable: she has to sit next to me while I shriek, yelp and bray.

Nobody stared at the Fighting Cocks — they were too busy rescuing themselves from helplessness.

So here we are, compressed into the room, shoehorned in.

The perspiration is dribbling.

Mr. Dowie warms up the audience (mentally that is) and then there is Louise Jones reading her poetry to a quitar accompaniment.

Small, intense and dressed in white she holds the audience well, but it is

difficult to forget that you are sweltering.

A short break and here he is dressed in a striped T shirt, red scarf and white trousers. His warm up promised a lot but he'd better be good.

These conditions are not funny.

He starts with a gas mask over his face, then moves into his ventriloquist routine.

Who is it he looks like? Extenuated, elevated. That's right Alice Cooper, the rock and roll star.

Very quickly Mr. John Dowie (he likes to be called that, although he very fashionably signs his letters with a small "j" and "d") proves to be an intelligent idiot (meant affectionately).

☆ Switch

He is into a routine that mixes the bizarre with the sly, the blue with pure clean humour that you could laugh at in front of your grandmother.

But **PLEASE** don't take her to see him unless she likes Monty Python or Up Sunday.

He's of that type.

He sings of his favourite things (Mary Poppins would have blushed to death) then he switches to this ventriloquist who has lost his voice but insists on performing.

Think about it!

Next he tells us that the Lone Ranger is deaf and substitutes the effeminate Lance for Big Bad John.

There were moments when the leakage won and I remembered how hard my stool was (that's something to use Mr. Dowie).

But they were very few.

For the record I was disappointed with the routine that gave Shakespearean speeches to actors with speech defects—but the idea is delightfully maniacal.

And the wood worker sketch belonged to the how-clever-that-is variety.

But the folk singer, the blues singer, the sweets instead of drugs—"I dropped 12 Cadbury's buttons last night"—were all very funny.

And the sketch on an Anglo - French television collaboration, now that we are in the Common Market, was ridiculously and amazingly effective.

I think he is a natural.

The story of a comedy gig in Moseley

Page 10 REDBRICK, September 29, 1978

CARNIVAL

Carnival is the name for Birmingham University's Rag, which takes place annually at the beginning of November. It involves a series of events and schemes aimed at raising money for the needy of Birmingham. Last year we raised over £6,000, which we donated to 23 different appeals. This year we can do better still.

Taking part in Carnival is an enjoyable and rewarding way of becoming involved in University life. Selling Ragmags, participating in sponsored events or joining our administrative committee are just a few of the ways of helping us — and we need as much help as possible.

If you would like to help us in any way please come to the Stall at Freshers Fayre on Sunday October 1st or to the Carnival Office on the second floor of the Union.

A REDBRICK EXCLUSIVE! Here is a preview of this year's rag mag. For other even better jokes, don't forget to buy a copy.

Crossing the street one morning, I was nearly run over by an old car packed with child passengers. Since I was on a zebra crossing at the time I shouted to the woman driving the car as she finally brought it to a halt, "Lady, don't you know when to stop?" Looking over her shoulder at the children, she replied coldly, "They aren't all mine, you know."

PASTBRICKS

15 years ago

— The front page of an eight page issue had the headline "Price rises hit Freshers". Tea had gone up over 30% from 3d to 4d; coffee from 4d to 5d. The Union now had to compete with the newly-opened Refectory, and was therefore losing £100 a week on catering. The previous year there had been a £700 a week surplus.
— The University's French Department took on a student with no arms. The previous year Birmingham, together with 4 other universities, had turned him down although he had had the same qualifications.
— Redbrick had won the award for Best Student Newspaper the year before, and the production team were complimenting themselves on its continuing excellence. The results of this year's competition are announced at the end of October. But although we take care not to count our chickens we can't help hoping . . . .
— New buildings opening at the time included the £1½ million Biology Block, the Commerce Block behind the library and High and Ridge Halls. The rest of the Vale Site was still being built. The Sports Centre was on the drawing board; so was a new theatre for the drama dept. This was never built — instead, students have to make do with the Muirhead.

10 years ago

— Accommodation was a problem then as now, and agaon the second and third years were hardest hit. The headline was: "Flats crisis" and the lodgings office lwas flooded with people who had left it all too late.
— Things weren't all roses for the first years either. In those distant days only about 400 of 1600 Freshers were women (the ratio now is down to about 1:2) so you can imagine the problems that must have caused.
— An extraordinary news story was reported: the time when someone pulled out the plug on the Vale Lake. Valves were opened at dead of night and the water simply drained away onto the Golf course. As far as we know, the culprits were never caught. That was the year when *all* the members of the Vale lost their deposits.

5 years ago

— The old Main Bar, on the site of today's shop, was closed over the vacation, and there were plans to build a mini-supermarket in the area. We're still waiting! The Main Bar was redecorated. Things don't change much.
— The first meeting of Senate (the Committee running the University) was cancelled because of fears of disruption by radical students. At the same time the army was not allowed a stall at the Freshers' Fair because of objections raised by left wing groups and pacifists. There's a moral there, but we can't think what it is.
— Matthew O'Callaghan was Welfare Chairman. He seems to have been here for years and years and years . . .

one year ago

— A very uneventful ossue. Worries about the increase in food prices filled the front page; the Vernon Hall had been redecorated (Priestley Hall should have been done this holiday but there was a cock-up). Chef's Specials saw the light of day and have proved to be a great success.
— News that a Fresher Flasher was on the loose in the Edgbaston Park Road area brought back memories of the Law Fac. Flasher who had been known to run along the tops of the desks during lectures, to the amusement of those in attendance. It seems he was asked to leave.
— Short of articles to print, as usual, desperate staff managed to find a board game called "Layopoly" in an old edition. This was reprinted, and proved to be offensive to many. This year we've managed to fill all our pages, next year — who knows, it may reappear.

Sundays, 8 p.m. at the Crown Hill Street.
city centre

grey cockfolk club

Free Small Ads

Have you something to sell? Or are you looking for something? or somebody? Lost something? Or just want to send someone a message? Do it through Redbrick. Every issue we will print all small ads from students, staff, or societies totally free of charge.

Advertisements or messages should be sealed in envelopes and either handed in at Union Reception or sent via Internal Post to Redbrick, The Union. Messages must be received by the Friday before publication; we cannot guarantee publication of those received after that date.

"WELK" needs a new editor. Applications, together with full Curriculum Vitae, should be placed in "We" Union Pigeon Hole.
Redbrick needs photographers and cartoonists. See us for details

Salad Days are here. New Salad Bar now open in the Union Coffee Bar. Support this new enterprise.

We regret to announce the closure of the Apathy Society due to lack of interest.

Sperm Donors Wanted for A.I.D. Paid for Inconvenience! Further details, contact Dr. S. Gregson, 643-1461 or collect a form from Welfare.

Wanted: talking parrot Long John Silver via UPH.

On behalf of CAMRA we are pleased to announce real ale is now avALEable in the Main Bar.

Problems? Loneliness? Contact NIteline 472-4616

Want to talk it over? Second Opinion — in Welfare Office Monday — Thrusday 4.30-6.30

Look out! Carnival is coming

LOOK

To eliminate unnecessary introductory conversation between Freshers. Redbrick this year is bringing out a special "Freshers Badge". Simply pin it on, and you won't have to talk to anyone for at least a fortnight. We were freshers once.

catastrophically and hilariously wrong. Life on the road with T&S was rarely conventional – Pete Chatfield again...

"The band's other roadie was Rob Cowlyn. On gig days George and Rob used to leave in the van with the gear just before us, then we'd follow in a car. One day we were going up the M6 passing Stafford when we saw this thing in the middle lane of the motorway. We suddenly realised it was George! Apparently he slid the door back to throw his fag end out, the door was ripped off its runners and Rob pulled onto the hard shoulder. Instinctively George jumped out and ran back to retrieve the door. When he realised where he was, he froze with fright until we happened to come along.

"T&S carried with their gear a piano, smaller than the usual, but not much lighter. George and I worked on building sites most days and we tended to be fairly fit. So we'd have to carry that thing up the back stairs at the Jolly Sailor in Tamworth and any other staircase that presented a challenge. Those were the days long before decent electric pianos.

"We once had a gig aboard a ship setting off from Barry Island along with a couple of other bands. We christened it the SS Seasick. Once we were underway and the merriment started, the gear was set up all ready for the sound check. The guys switched the gear on and the ship stopped – we'd overloaded the electrics!"

In those Wild West days when diversity had a wholly different meaning and taking the knee was what one did to tie shoelaces, Tea and Symphony had a genuine social conscience and did not shy away from displaying it.

Their second album was called Jo Sago. The gatefold sleeve was taken over by a photograph of a room, painted white, with a white carpet, white furniture – and a young black man, seated, cradling his head on his arm on the table and clearly most unhappy. It doesn't take a psychiatrist to decipher the message. The man's name is Jo Sago. He's a black man in a white man's world which he finds confusing or depressing or, most probably, both.

He lives – or would, if he actually existed – on Ladypool Road which starts in the increasingly rundown former red-light area of Balsall Heath and runs south into Moseley. Picking up the liner notes from the album, "Ladypool Road is brimming with the less industrious portion of the Balsall Heath overspill and rehabilitation centres for the victims of the Varna Road clearance schemes. The first residential outcry was against the wild colour schemes that the immigrant newcomers chose for their immediate stretches of pavement and the candy-striped lamp-posts that appeared in the vicinity.

"The painted public monument exhibitions and the ever-thickening smells of over-stewed Jamaican jumping beans, boiled brown rice and high-octane home-stilled bootleg rum soon drove the less

adaptable residents and their distant colonial memories away from the parish and overnight their scuttled mansions became adventure playgrounds for Jo Sago, his friends and others like him. Of the people who stayed, many have taken to sipping carrot juice, eating their potatoes sweet and enjoying Caribbean pleasures."

Side 1 of the album is Jo Sago, a play in music featuring six songs about Jo and his chums, what they get up to, what they eat, what they smoke, and it's fascinating stuff, albeit with rather more than a whiff of smouldering fine herbs.

Ladypool in the 1970s was a wondrous place, full of riotous colour, loud music of Caribbean and Asian origin, and an unbelievable selection of affordable eating houses and coffee houses. April Phillips, wife of Tea and Symphony's Nigel, remembers vividly Adil's in nearby Stoney Lane:

"Plastic cloths. No cutlery. Wonderful food. Later became very popular with BBC people, but I remember it long before that."

The key element in Ladypool life was the music – and Don Christie's Blue Beat Record Store was at the very hub, specialising in black music, riding the changes from rock steady to ska to reggae and all the offshoots along the way. The words "The Reggae Specialist" were emblazoned across the shop's red and white frontage and musicians came from miles around to listen to the latest 45s imported from Jamaica, meet other musicians, have a little taste and maybe some smoke. UB40's Robin Campbell recalls ganja being smoked openly in the shop while the music boomed from the speakers.

Ladypool Road had a past and was to enjoy a future. In 1940 two Yemenis purchased a cottage and folks who were children at the times remembered the excitement when they encountered them out and about. If that was the start of Ladypool's cosmopolitan heritage, how about today when it sits at the centre of Birmingham's world-famous Balti Triangle? And not only that. Terry Poole adds, "Lots of old-style curry houses have now morphed into ice-cream parlours – it makes Ladypool Road and Stoney Lane still vibrant today."

REDBRICK, September 29, 1978   Page 7

BEFORE YOUR TIME...

One of the many complaints which we at Redbrick receive immediately after an issue goes on sale is that there is a serious lack of new items. This year we hope to solve this problem by encouraging the whole student body to search out and compile news stories. However, for newcomers to the University we are printing here a summary of the main new items which we included last year. Many of these will doubtless recur this year, but it's as well to be prepared . . .

October

Stories included the rising prices of meals in the Union, and the continuing problem of cowboy insurance salesmen. There was concern over the number of students being duped into taking out expensive life assurance policies which they didn't really need. Later in the year some firms started sending unsolicited letters to Hall residents. This will probably recur this year, so be warned: sign *nothing* without *reading* and *understanding* it.

November

The most important event was the election of a Vice-President External. There had been two elections the previous summer term: in the first the successful candidate had been disqualified for allegedly printing too many leaflets (there are strict quotas). The second candidate resigned after a few hours, and a second election was necessary. This was won by the now-famous White Dalek, but he had to resign through pressure of work. The third election was won by Ian Brown, who continued in office until last July. The post is now held by Andy Masheter.

Ian Brown

The black-outs caused some concern when the Queen Elizabeth Hospital was apparently without power for several minutes. Carnival took place but there were complaints that students failed to put enough effort into collecting money on Procession Day (when it poured with rain). Redbrick staff refused to print a full issue until their office was improved, particularly the lighting. There was the first story on the University's plans to phase out the Educational Counselling Unit. This is run by Dr Janek Wankowski to help students who have trouble adapting to new teaching methods. An article by Dr Wankowski appears in this issue.

December

The University's proposals on the future of the E.C.U. became clearer — they wanted to transfer it to smaller premises with a reduced staff — tantamount to closure. An independent assessor was appointed, and, swayed we hope by a Union campaign led by President Matthew O'Callaghan, he decided to recommend the retention and possible expansion of the service.

There was a General Meeting on the Palestinian Problem, which had to be held in the Concourse Lounge due to an administrative cock-up. As befits a moderate University like Birmingham, the motion ultimately passed was one simply to encourage further discussion between the two groups. A motion to ban the Jewish Society on Campus was soundly defeated.

Quentin Crisp

January

Guild Council was unable to meet through lack of quorum for the first but not the last time that year; even after the January elections there were still many vacancies. The Chairman of the External Affairs Committee chained himself to Pebble Mill to protest about lack of media coverage for a strike in Turkey. The front of the University Centre flaked off and had to be replaced. An experimental Open meeting on Accommodation attracted less than 50 people.

February

Quentin Crisp spoke in the Debating Hall one lunchtime. He was originally meant to speak in the Council Chamber, with Sir Idwal Puch (the Ombudsman) in the Deb. Hallm but owing to his popularity the venues had to be reversed.

The National Front marched through the centre of Birmingham. There was concern at the number of bicycles being stolen from the campus: at one stage it reached an average of four a week.

The BBC filmed a musical on campus, which culminated in a free concert in the Great Hall starring Sonja Kristina. It was shown in late May, and was *terrible*. Fun to see them filming, though.

March

British Rail forgot to take the Red Star Parcel containing Redbrick's copy off the train at Birmingham and sent it northwards — no thanks to them that week. There was a grants march through the centre of Birmingham; originally scheduled for London it had to be moved due to a blanket ban on marches in London after NF troubles. Presidential elections took place, with the usual low polling figure of about 25%.

Sonja Kristina

May

Lecturers were threatening to refuse to mark final examinations, and so stop the awarding of degrees unless the government corrected a pay anomaly. This moral blackmail was successful and the dispute was settled half-way through the exam period. The first news trickled through about plans to demolish the Gun Barrels, the nearest pub to the University. The University Railway Station was opened. Proposals to "rationalise" the Metallurgy depts leaked out; this subject is bound to continue through the year. Basically it seems the University is trying to do things behind the students' backs.

June

Exams came and went; so did the summer. The Vice-Chancellor was made a Life Peer, and became a Baron; the Open University made threating noises when students at Birmingham were found to be using codes allocated to Leeds. President Roy Evans was elected N.U.S. Area Secretary. The year ground to an end. And now another is just beginning . . .

WHAT'S ON.

Are you organising an event? Redbrick will give you a *free* listing in our "What's On" section, provided that the relevant information is provided well in advance (preferably at the beginning of each term). Latest copy date is usually Friday before publication; we cannot guarantee publication of items received after that date.

Friday 29th September
7.30   GTG presents an Ionesco plat. Deb Hall.
7.30   String Quartet in TV lounge.
8.30   Disco in Founders Room.
8.30   Stallion (rock band) in Main Bar.

Saturday 30th September
12.00 – 2.00 Folk/Jazz in Main Bar
2.00   Cartoon films in TV lounge
7.30   Midland Red Theatre in TV lounge
7.30   Freshers' Debate in Council Chamber: "This House believes that the future of Universities lies in student power".
8.00   Freshers' Concert in Debating Hall with School Sports and No Mystery
8.00   Disco in Founders Room
8.00   Folk Concert with Mithras in Priestley Hall

Sunday 1st October
1.30   Motor Club Car Trials in West Car Park
7.00   Film in Deb. Hall: 'That's Entertainment II'

Tuesday 3rd October
8.00   Folk Club: Bill Caddick – singer/songwriter. Mixed lounge.

Thursday 5th October
7.30   Debate in Council Chamber: "This House believes that Nationalised Industries waste taxpayers' money."

Friday 6th October
7.30   Introductory evening for new postgraduates. Founders Room.

Tuesday 10th October
8.00   Ceileidh (Barn Dance) Folk Club. See Folk Club for venue.

WHAT'S OFF

CINEMAS

ABC, New Street
Until Saturday: Housecalls
from Sunday: Silent Partner

ABC 123, Bristol Road
1   Playbirds
2   Heaven Can Wait
3   Convoy

GAUMONT COLMORE CIRCUS
Wild Geese

ODEON, Queensway
Turning Point

ABC, Selly Oak *(70p with Guild Card)*
closed until Sunday
from Sunday: Thank God It's Friday

FOLK CLUB

Hi there, it's me, the organiser of the Campus Folk Club, to tell you all about the wonderful guests such as Fred Wedlock, John & Sue Kirkpatrick etc. we have booked at the club. We function every Tuesday night in the Mixed Lounge next to the Mermaid Bar in the Union. Since we're near the bar and since the guests are all superb there will be no possible excuse for not spending a drunken enjoyable evening at the Folk Club. Floor singers are always welcome, so see you!

Mick Bisike

FRIENDS OF THE EARTH

For all those interested in conservation and various ecological activities, a university-based Friends of the Earth group has just been formed. We will be keeping in contact with Birmingham FOE as well as organising events and discussions of our own. Things will be getting under way this term, and additional support will be more than welcome. Anyone interested should visit the FOE stall at the Freshers Fair or contact Jo Bradford via the Union pigeon holes in Reception.

Barmy Barry, pioneer DJ
Photo by Jim Simpson

Chapter 8
Djs, dogs and skating on thin ice

Ansells – one of Birmingham's prime breweries

The 1970s saw the rise of the personality disc jockey, for sound financial reasons according to Barmy Barry: "The clubs would pay maybe £40 for a group, £10 for a disc jockey, then they found people were coming in for the DJ as much as the groups, so they'd drop down from three groups on the bill to two and a DJ to one and a DJ, then maybe to just a DJ."

And Barry should know! He claims to be the first of the disc jockeys, the man Jimmy Saville learned his craft from (only in his turntable manner, of course!). Unfortunately Barry's attempt to get his claim into the *Guinness Book of Records* failed, but it's difficult to imagine who came before the 16-year-old Barry Cary in Manchester in 1957.

Barry was the first on the Birmingham scene, by the 1970s working all the Fewtrell clubs, The Opposite Lock, the Rum Runner and so on, gradually joined by other DJs such as Erskine T., doing the same circuit week and week about with

Barry, and Peter York at the Mecca, Dale End. Ask Barry what style of music he favoured and the answer is, "Everything! I never wanted to be a specialist."

Where does the "Barmy" come from? Some guy in Cheadle Hulme in Barry's early days, John Eaton, who said, "You ought to have a stage name. You're a bit bloody nuts!" So Barmy Barry he became – well, he did dye his hair pink, green and blue and wear odd socks, offering a fiver to anyone who caught him wearing a matched pair.

The Shoop upstairs at the Golden Eagle projected a different image. Described by sociologist (and Dirty Stop Out) Dick Hebdige as "the one hip place that wasn't in any of the nightclubs", to Eileen Vichare it was "the highlight of the week. Dead broke, but we had a great night out."

Mark Stephen Reeves has vivid recollections of The Shoop: "The Shoop was the highlight of my week. I come from a northern soul background so my dancing was at about twice

NITES

Birmingham boasts a surprisingly large number of nightclubs. Restrictions, access, drink prices and style may vary tremendously, but by and large the sensibly dressed, reasonably behaved customer can get into any club with a minimum of fuss and at a fair price.

The City Centre features something like ten niteries with many concentrated in the area between John Bright Street and Bristol Street. Brum's veteran club entrepreneur Edward Fewtrell seems to have taken over half of John Bright Street and has serious intentions regarding the remainder. Adjacent to his always-popular disco bars - **Boogies Brasserie** and **Edwards No.7** - you find a brace of always buzzing clubs - **Boogies** and **Edwards No.8** - where the more youthful end of nightclub clientele can be found and which both offer student half-price admission on production of N.U.S. cards, and in conjunction with their sister-venues **Boogies Brasserie, Number 7** and **Paramount**, currently have 100,000 half-bottles of French wine to distribute among their female patrons. Live bands are an increasingly popular feature at **Number 8.**

Around the corner on Smallbrook Queensway, **The Millionaire** fronts onto **Pagoda Park.** The Millionaire is a very successful fun palace; Competitions, promotion nights and contests are a regular feature - look out for the upcoming Mistergram Contest where local male kissogramists vie with each other for the title. Parties of students are offered discounts on all bookings and it is currently planning to re-introduce special student passes, which allow the holder entrance for just 50p on Monday, Tuesday and Wednesday.

The **Pagoda Park** features stunning decor rather in the manner of a Japanese garden, complete with Bonsai trees, bamboo bridge and an actual waterfall. Although there are no special rates for students at Pagoda Park they are in fact very welcome. The nightclub is owned by First Leisure, who also own what is claimed to be Europe's most spectacular nite spot. **The Dome** can hold 2,000 people and is open on Monday, Thursday, Friday and Saturday. The club's many features include mammoth video screens and a strongly student-oriented policy. On October 14th, **The Dome** will feature a Freshers Party Night featuring **Working Week** and **Furniture** live on stage. Discounted drinks will be the order of the day, as they will at the subsequent Tuesday Students nights, with live bands and a £1 entry charge.

Sited in Hurst Street, **The Powerhouse** - a seven night a week niterie catering for the younger nightclub element. **The Powerhouse** programme is invariably action-packed with some of the zaniest parties in town. Fifty pence is the price tag for Mondays special student nights, which were a smash hit last season. Two more long-established city niteries both make themselves available for students party booking. They are **Tressines** in Newhall Street and **Snobs** on Paradise Circus. Snobs also offer an any-night reduced admission to bearers of any students I.D. card.

Bonkers is the newest addition to Brum's coterie of nightclubs. "The customer is always wrong" is their proudly-held motto, while recent stunts included a fairly serious attempt to jump half-a-dozen supine customers by some bloke on a very real 500cc motorbike, plus some of the wildest cabaret acts you can every hope to see - or avoid, dependent upon your sensibility! Although **Bonkers** is too new to have yet formulated a policy, it is fairly obvious that the place is well in tune with the more frivolous of student needs. The party booking deal is well worth checking out.

Moving westwards along Broad Street, the first port of call is **Bobby Browns, The Club** on Gas Street. Built alongside the canal, **Bobby Browns** enjoyed past glory as **The Opposite Lock** - now tastefully refurbished, it is indeed very, very swish. No student policy as such, though all are welcome. Not a stones throw away is **Burberries** on Broad Street, newly opened but already a fave watering house of Brums glitterati. Live music features every Tuesday in what is essentially an over 21's spot, though party bookings can effectively reduce the admission price to £1.

Still travelling west you would reach a duo of clubs based in Auchinleck Square at Five Ways. **Maximillians** is a cosy and friendly club which is a little quiet at the moment following a change of ownership. It offers half price party bookings for all students. **Faces International** is a large club that offers half price admission to all students proffering a N.U.S. card.

On the Hagley Road, a little further out from town is **Liberty's** - a superbly

appointed niterie that would be a credit to Paris, London or Rome - let alone dear old Brum. Monday night is live jazz night at **Liberty's** and only £2 admission.

Birmingham's oldest - and possibly most comfortable - niteclub is **The Elbow Room** - situated in High Street, Aston. Relaxed and low key, it tends to be the haunt of muzos and music biz people. Low on glitter.

So that's about it, students of Elektrik Nightclubbing. Don't fritter away your cash on books and eating and rent - get out, get up and get down.

the speed of the music, but I didn't much care how ridiculous I looked. I remember the adrenaline rush of the dance, the bottles of Carlsberg Special and wringing out my soaking wet T-shirt at the end of the night."

Michael Horseman was in charge at The Shoop, later joined by Pete King who takes up the story:

"It had a long history before my involvement, but we certainly had a great sound system! It was a melting pot for

---

The DJs at Bogart's were highly influential, too, in opening Dirty Stop Outs' ears to different music.

---

all kinds of music and people. It was like a perfect world for about three hours on a Thursday night at the Eagle. Sometimes we spread our wings and did away gigs, but we got closed down at Barbarella's one night supporting Hamilton Bohannon for daring to light spliffs while spinning the discs."

The number of DJs from the 1970s still remembered with admiration is huge – Nicky Steele, Robin Valk, Nick Hennegan of BRMB, Mark Roy – with Michael Horseman one of the most popular:

"I can remember virtually everyone I met in the late 1970s asking if I had heard Michael Horseman as they rated him so highly." (Carol Maye)

Mark Stephen Reeves even paid him the ultimate compliment of copying him:

"I was the resident DJ at the Dumas Express upstairs at the Opposite Lock on Thursday nights. I'm not suggesting I was one of the best, but I initially borrowed the style of music I played from Mike before I developed the self-confidence to own my own style.

"Erskine T at Mothers was a great DJ and a top bloke – incredibly knowledgeable. I first met him when he was working at the Diskery on Hurst Street. I thought I knew a lot about soul music, but he was like a walking computer of soul knowledge."

The DJs at Bogart's were highly influential, too, in opening Dirty Stop Outs' ears to different music. Ruth Cheshire is typical:

"I may not have heard of the Allmans and the Doobies without Bogart's. I was more into progressive music. It was the American stuff that was a revelation to me – and Robin Trower. I don't think I'd have stumbled into him without Bogart's.'

Situated next to Birmingham's Wholesale Market on Pershore Street was Silver

Blades, the city's premier ice-skating rink, opened by Mecca in 1965. In school holidays it became a teenager's paradise, a place to hang out, bring your date, skate some and laugh off the bruises, but it was much more than that. Midway up one of the rink's straights was a stage with a DJ in place and often live soul, funk and disco bands, sometimes surprisingly big names. Musicians were often confounded by playing to an audience that went flying past them far too quickly to show the expected enthusiasm for the band's performance.

Silver Blades was home to the Birmingham Mohawks Speed Skating Club and later to Newtown-born Olympic champion speed skater Wilf O'Reilly. The more well-heeled could take figure skating lessons at the then not inconsiderable rate of £3.25 for a half-hour session, but most folks settled for clinging to the side-rails and watching the skaters fly by before tackling a plate of chips drowned in tomato ketchup.

Below Silver Blades was the club and dance hall Heartbeat, memorably described by Pete King as "lots of snogging and Wrigley's Spearmint".

HIGH ON SPINACH

'THE MUSICAL ARMS' ~ SHERLOCK STREET HOME OF POPEYE'S

IF YOU haven't yet sampled the delights of POPEYE'S, you'd better hurry because it's going fast. The site of the Birmingham Arms is to be redeveloped, so in its present form, Popeye's days are numbered. Still, there's time enough to get down there one of these Saturday nights and let it rip with the bunch - and even if it is doomed to close soon, the chances are a new home for this alternative entertainment scene will be found.

The upstairs room at the Arms has been well-known around the town for its Jazz sessions every Friday; the management have been into letting things happen up above. So, when Frankie Spencer and friends approached the pub, they got a good deal at a fair price. For a start, the entrance price is as low as you could expect for a shoestring club which survives on performers just showing up, with a little encouragement from the lads. For 30p you're likely to get rock, folk, theatre, poetry, lightshow (from the talented Fred and Alan), a bar laid-on, and the constant promise of some surprise appearance by visiting musicians. Idle Race, Trev Burton, Graham Bond, Tea & Symphony are a few of the people who just came and played.

The accent really is on what naturally happens - if you want to play, then play; if you want to do a mime, read your poems, go ahead and do it. Rumour has it that even Frankie doesn't know what's on until maybe a couple of minutes before. You can imagine the sort of problems that this kind of free policy might bring, and sure there have been set-backs.

A few weeks ago, plainclothes officers came and had a nose round and since that time there have been difficulties with the extension license which was previously granted every other week on a Saturday. Now we have to wait for a magistrate's decision which has been put off more than once already.

But despite these small troubles, the club has been a big success. It lost a bit of bread early on when audiences averaged about 50, but these days many more people have come to realise that there is something going on down in Digbeth and everything has picked up.

Something which has certainly helped the scene at Popeye's is Frankie Spencer's experience in this kind of area. Two years ago he was connected with the Paradiso in Amsterdam, helping with the community gigs there, finding himself in the middle of a huge new experiment in alternative living and entertainment. Working with the lady of the house, Anna-Maria, he got involved with the all-nighters, films, the cheap and free food programmes and lots of the other activities around that very high time. Perhaps one day he'll find a way to put on Council subsidized concerts in Birmingham but personally I'd rather see Popeye's and a few more like it sprout out of the city's backstreets.

Even back then people were worrying about losing the British pub

AS BULLDOZERS DEMOLISH THE OLD DRINKING HALLS, TONY SCHRAMM RECALLS

PUBS WE HAVE LOST

When they chopped down the Woodman it left a pretty wide gap in a lot of lives. It's clientele moped around, lost, speechless. So indeed was I although in my case this had more to do with the fact that I only ever visited the place once, thought it a dump, and trotted round to the Cambridge. In fact I was only made aware of its passing when, homeless and lonely, the gregarious ex-Woodman band drifted round to the Greyhound. Squeezed out, I sought refuge in my local, the Bull in Moseley when people still went there for the beer.

Memoirs are always boring but if you really want a bad time then you couldn't do worse than drop into your local jazz or folk club. For a whole evening of time enhanced reminicences of the 'remember the Fishgutters Arms-now there was a pub' ilk, just make for the bar. Here in a huddle, their sleeves soaking up beer off the counter, you'll find four or five inelligible bachelors, looking uncomfortably like me, except that they'll be wearing suits, gently swaying fowards and then backwards as though tied to each other by elastic. Buy a round and be sure to end up missing the last bus. The barman will start clearing the pub, you'll notice the time and start to leave. It's all right, 'you'll be reassured, the drummer goes home your way, he'll give you a lift.' With the last bus long since gone, it invariably

'SQUEEZED OUT, I SOUGHT REFUGE IN THE BULL, MOSELEY, WHEN PEOPLE WENT FOR THE BEER'

transpires that by the time the drummer has finally managed to stow away his kit there's room for just one more, and she lives at Kingswinford. And still they pressure you, you should be all right. It's no trouble at all getting a lift down the Walsall Rd. Dead easy. No trouble at all. They all live in Kings Norton and the accuracy of the information supplied by your new found friends proves to be the usual standard.

There's a repetitious list of pubs gone. And pubs going; The Drovers Arms; The Cambridge; The King Edward the seventh or eighth, now carpeted and catering for 'private functions', as indeed is the Crown in Corporation St. & the Warwick Castle at the side of Aston University: Now that was

probably the best room of all, and Danny Pawson, for one, has never sounded as good since. The only redeeming feature about the place now though is that its present manager is Gerry Keene who used to run the Salutation.

Take the Salutation. Now for most people this place evokes only the fondest of memories. They can remember only being packed solid in order to catch visits by the real thing from New Orleans on a hot summers day, when they met more people they'd forgotten they knew than they would at their brothers wedding. Me, I remember only a cold insanitary slum where I felt embarassed whenever I had to explain to someone that we were actually charging for admission. I've even heard some attempt at nostalgia over the Birmingham Arms. This could be the stumper however, I was there for the last night a few weeks back, and in fact it was one of the best sessions in the club's history. The place was packed and everyone seemed to enjoy themselves, but by this time the tatty, run down, dilapidated state of the place had left me hating it.

It has always seemed to me strange that people reminisce nostalgically over pubs, long gone and by the majority unmourned. The reason is simple. They don't differentiate between the music and the venue. In itself this is hardly surprising as most of them rarely even enter the clubrooms, preferring to stay in the bar and follow the proceedings second hand. What Birmingham needs is not to keep redundant and obsolete pubs like the Salutation standing but for one of the breweries to open up a cheap, unpretentious room, just off the city centre, (along Broad St. say), catering solely for live jazz, folk, rock and blues. This would probably do more for the local music than any number of subsidies.
See you in the Windsor.

Among all the happy memories of Silver Blades and Heartbeat, Mark Stephen Reeves strikes a discordant note:

"Went precisely once. Almost got my ass kicked by three guys one of whom accused me of eyeing up his girlfriend. I had no idea who his girlfriend was, so couldn't definitively say I was innocent of said crime. Barely escaped with a few scratches and bruises. Never went back."

The emotional scars have clearly not healed, but on a happier note Luke Skyscraper James played his part in getting Silver Blades a mention on national radio:

"My old band Fashion's last single was called *Silver Blades*. It was about a night out at the rink. John Peel played it on Radio 1."

Oddly enough horse racing didn't move to Perry Barr – every other form of racing known to man or beast seemed to find a home there!

George Beamish gives us something of a survey of what he rather quaintly calls "watering holes" in 1970s Birmingham:

"Back in the day, about 1972 or so, there used to be several below-ground watering holes in Birmingham. Some were proper pubs, The Costermonger I seem to recall, some were clubs, some that perhaps didn't feature in a list of licensed premises.

"Saturday afternoons we sometimes used to go to a club in a side street in the city centre. We called it The Incognito. You had to have a tie to get in, I wore mine as a hat band. If you didn't have a tie, you could buy one on the door. Downstairs there was a bar, a stage and tables. The bar wasn't open all afternoon, but you could drink until the bands had finished which was probably about half past four.

"I only really remember one band I saw there who were on quite regularly – that was The Steve Gibbons Band, the whole place on their feet shouting 'Speed Kills!' which was their closing number. I spent a few happy afternoons there before moving on to whatever the evening had in store."

Do it youself

Night clubber Carole Williams clearly felt so much at home in her regular haunt, Romeo and Juliet's, that she felt able to complain to the manager about what she felt was the poor quality of some of the acts appearing there. His response was to offer her the chance to perform there herself. Which she did, one Saturday evening, delivering a 30-minute set

that included *Don't Cry for Me, Argentina* and *I Will Survive*. Reportedly her performance was well received, but there is no record of whether or not she was re-booked.

Bromford Bridge and Perry Barr

Sadly by the time the 1970s came round a tradition of more than 200 years horse racing in Birmingham had come to an end. Racing historian Chris Pitt tells us the first horse racing meet in Birmingham was in 1747, exact location unknown. After a century and a half's nomadic existence, horse racing settled at Bromford Bridge in 1894. However, by the 1960s, race-goers seemed to prefer the more rural surroundings of Stratford or Warwick and the last meeting at Bromford Bridge came in 1965. Collectors of trivia enjoy the fact that Lester Piggott rode the locally named Selly Oak to victory in one of the last races.

Oddly enough horse racing didn't move to Perry Barr – every other form of racing known to man or beast seemed to find a home there! The only problem was working out which stadium to go to. In the 1970s not only the humans, bikes and dogs were on the move. Let's start with Birchfield Harriers. The famous athletics club had been using the Alexander Sports Ground – now known as the Perry Barr Stadium – since 1929, but in 1977 decamped to the confusingly named Alexander Stadium. Meanwhile the old Perry Barr Stadium, together with Hall Green Stadium a long established venue for greyhound and speedway racing, was re-titled the Birchfield Ladbroke Stadium in honour of its new owners who soon demonstrated their commitment by selling the site to developers. So, where Alan Hunt and Mick the Miller once raced, shoppers now jostle for position at the One Stop Shopping Centre.

But that wasn't the end for the Brummies speedway team or dog racing in Perry Barr. In 1990 the former home of Birchfield Harriers was re-cycled as a home for greyhound racing and speedway. So, just like in the 1970s, the Perry Barr Stadium exists alongside the Alexander – just not in the same place!

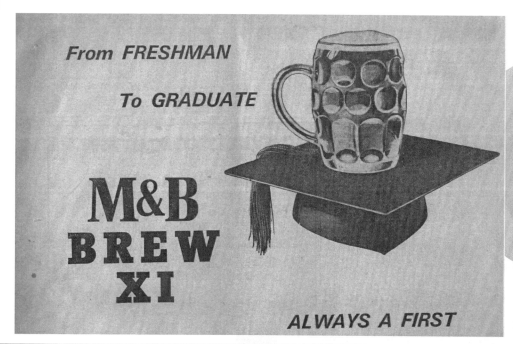

 **MAY DAY**

!FESTIVAL!

at

Digbeth Civic Hall

KID'S KARNIVAL

MUSIC

Bar and Food all day

Crafts

MARCH & RALLY
Dr. David Owen M.P.
Mel Chavannes
Mike Thomas M.P.
J. Joshi
Geoffrey Drain

Exhibitions

Theatre

& lots more

...Monday....May....1st.... Tickets £1·00 OAPs & Under 16s 25p

---

STOP WINDSCALE

DEMO   SATURDAY 29th APRIL
Hyde Park – Trafalgar Square
Make it a cheap day out in London and join the demo.
F.O.E. arranging special rail excursion from
Wolverhampton, Birmingham and Coventry
Return: £3.00 Block bookings of 20 plus. £2.50
Cheques to F.O.E., Birmingham.
54 Allison St., B5.   632 6909
P.S. Also, Wednesday 26th April, a new Danish film:–
"NO MORE NUCLEAR POWER STATIONS",
Dr. Johnson House, Bull Street, 8.0 p.m.

STUDENTS UNION, UNIVERSITY OF
ASTON, GOSTA GREEN, BIRMINGHAM.

RACE RELATIONS
AND CIVIL LIBERTIES

Wednesday

MAY 3 AT 7.30 P.M.

Speakers: Ted Ratnaraja – David Mc Carthy

For details contact:
National Council for Civil Liberties,
West Midlands Group,
12 Wake Green Road, Birmingham 13.

THEOSOPHICAL
SOCIETY

THERE IS NO RELIGION HIGHER THAN TRUTH

"The One, transcendant to all thought, form and
differentiations, the universal source, the end and
the beginning - the One is the central philosophic
vision of the great mystics. In that vision, men have
for centuries found exaltations of spirit and
philosophic beauty.

The conditions of a solitary bird are five:
The first, that it flies to the highest point;
The second, that it does not suffer company,
not even of its own kind;
The third, that it aims its beak to the skies;
The fourth, that it does not have a definite
colour;
The fifth, that it sings very softly.

St. John of the Cross.

Room 4, Friends Hall, Farm Street, Lozells.
Sundays, 6.30 p.m.

Chapter 9
Rep on the move

REPERTORY THEATRE, BIRMINGHAM

In 1971 an era came to an end in Birmingham theatre. The Birmingham Repertory Theatre was founded by Barry Jackson in 1913: a 464-seat auditorium crammed into a tiny site on Station Street. Its reputation was out of all proportion to its size, the theatre where the careers of the likes of Laurence Olivier and Paul Scofield started – or, in the late 1950s and 1960s, Albert Finney and Derek Jacobi. In 1963 Jacobi starred in the productions of the only three Shakespeare plays the Rep had not staged – total Shakespeare in 50 years!

"I have fond memories of the Rep in Station Street. I think it was a trip with the Brownies when I was about nine. *Midsummer Night's Dream*. We were taken backstage and my lasting memory is of Titania and her make-up. Fascinated me and, I think, was the start of my love of theatre." – April Phillips

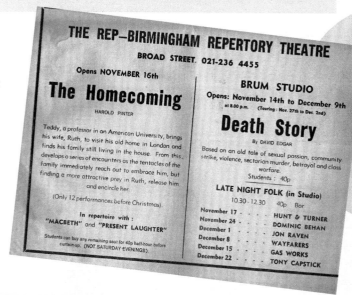

THE REP–BIRMINGHAM REPERTORY THEATRE
BROAD STREET. 021-236 4455

Opens NOVEMBER 16th

The Homecoming
HAROLD PINTER

Teddy, a professor in an American University, brings his wife, Ruth, to visit his old home in London and finds his family still living in the house. From this develops a series of encounters as the tentacles of the family immediately reach out to embrace him, but finding a more attractive prey in Ruth, release him and encircle her.

(Only 12 performances before Christmas).

In repertoire with :
"MACBETH" and "PRESENT LAUGHTER"

Students can buy any remaining seat for 40p half-hour before curtain-up. (NOT SATURDAY EVENINGS).

BRUM STUDIO
Opens: November 14th to December 9th
at 8.00 p.m.   (Touring : Nov. 27th to Dec. 2nd)

Death Story
By DAVID EDGAR

Based on an old tale of sexual passion, community strike, violence, sectarian murder, betrayal and class warfare.
Students : 40p

LATE NIGHT FOLK (in Studio)
10.30 - 12.30   40p   Bar

November 17	HUNT & TURNER
November 24	DOMINIC BEHAN
December 1	JON RAVEN
December 8	WAYFARERS
December 15	GAS WORKS
December 22	TONY CAPSTICK

The Rep had a lighter side, too, notably the frequent Christmas performances of *1066 and All That*, the immensely silly musical revue based on Sellar and Yeatman's nutty pseudo-history. It was *1066 and All That* that was chosen as the last Birmingham Repertory Theatre production at The Old Rep (though the theatre, of course, remains open). In those days actors often remained with the repertory company for years and the cast included several Birmingham favourites, better known for their long-running television parts, including Jane Freeman, Ivy in *Last of the Summer Wine*, and the archetypal Birmingham actor, Paul Henry, born in Aston, best known as that great Brummie icon, Benny in *Crossroads*.

While the Rep was shifting its site, Birmingham's oldest music venue carried on regardless – at least until the 1990s

1066 and All That opened on December 16th 1970 and closed on April 3rd 1971. Six months later the New Rep opened on Broad Street, main auditorium twice the capacity of the Old Rep, studio an added extra. And – what do you know? – the cast of *First Impressions*, a musical version of *Pride and Prejudice* starring Patricia Routledge, included Jane

STAGE STAGE

The Alexandra Theatre
Suffolk Street, Queensway. Telephone: 021-643 1231
The Alex is currently the prime venue for touring productions, generally taking on single week runs. The Alex is a decidedly middle-brow theatre, and seems to specialise in 'hilarious farces' along with assorted musicals and the regular extravagant panto. Every now and then a slightly more stimulating item appears - recently Nell Dunn's **'Steaming'** and Ira Levin's **'Veronica's Room'**. It's a roomy comfortable theatre, although the foyer and lounge are actually somewhat more opulent than the auditorium itself.
Student Discount: Half price on Saturdays.

The Hippodrome
Hurst Street. Telephone: 021-622 7486
The Hippodrome is the other main venue for touring companies, and is one of the longest serving theatres in the city. It has only recently undergone a massive exterior renovation to bring its façade up to scratch with the splendour of its interior and auditorium. The Hippodrome has earned a superior reputation for presentations such as the regular visits of the Royal Ballet, the Welsh National Opera, the National Theatre, and most recently, the Bolshoi Ballet. Appealing to a wider market The Hippodrome offers such theatre-filling fare as 'Joseph and the Amazing Technicolour Dreamcoat', 'Jesus Christ Superstar' and the forthcoming 1987 production of 'Evita', whilst there have also been several West End Premieres such as 'Cabaret', and one-man shows from the likes of Phil Cool.
There are two sizeable bars but be warned, trying to escape from the stalls during the interval requires superhuman speed and reflexes.
Student Discount: Available on most shows.

Birmingham Repertory Theatre
Broad Street. Telephone: 021-236 4455
The Rep is Birmingham's Premiere - It boasts the most visually impressive building and bids fair to take the honours in terms of its repertoire and cast too. A risk-taking programme caters for both mainstream and more upmarket audiences, with the likes of 'Charley's Aunt' nestling alongside Moliere's 'The Miser' or 'A Man For All Seasons', in the Main House, with the Studio Theatre scoring triumphs with Bristol Express' 'Elsie And Norm's Macbeth' and Foco Novo's 'The Lower Depths'. Whilst looking ahead, their new season includes 'Outskirts' by Hanif Kureshi - the author of 'My Beautiful Laundrette'. The Rep also stages regular Sunday concerts with a Jazz Bias and

Unen...
then Birm...
you! FOR JUST...
REPCARD whi...
for any Birmi...
Main House o...
evenings and...
REPCARD is v...
apply at the...

REMEM...
No other co...
Students, U...

for just
£1

CRESCENT THEATRE
CUMBERLAND STREET (OFF BROAD STREET)
BIRMINGHAM B1 2JA

11th–25th October 1986 at 7.30pm
SHE STOOPS TO CONQUER
by Oliver Goldsmith
The battle of the sexes was never funnier

24th Jan–7th February 1987 at 7.30pm
CIDER WITH ROSIE
by Laurie Lee
Adapted by Nick Darke
A man's memories of his countryside childhood

28th February–14th March 1987 at 7.30pm
MEASURE FOR MEASURE
by William Shakespeare
Exposé of a depraved society

4th–18th April 1987 at 7.30pm
THE FALL AND REDEMPTION OF MAN
by John Bowen
Creation to judgement day – an unforgettable dramatic and spiritual experience

27th April–2nd May 1987 for 6 nights only at 7.30pm
BINGO
by Edward Bond
Shakespeare's final years in retirement!

6th–20th June 1987 at 7.30pm
PERFECTLY FRANK
A musical tribute to American songwriter –
Frank 'Guys and Dolls' Loesser

BOX OFFICE: 021-643 5858
TICKET SHOP 021-643 2514

is the touring home of the Ballet Rambert. Productions have included several U.K. and World Premieres, and the company has further advanced its reputation for experimentation and bold scheduling by such staging.
The Rep also has the benefit of a full-fledged brasserie and restaurant at front of house, and you don't have to attend a performance to go there. It's worth noting that the Rep has a good Student discount scheme for students, called the Rep Card, which costs just £1 and entitles you to Half Price Tickets for any main/studio production, except Saturday evenings and the Christmas performances and is valid for a year.

The Triangle
Aston University Arts & Media Centre.
Telephone: 021-359 3979
The productions here are of a uniformly high standard, both from visiting companies and from the Triangle's own offspring The Big Brum Theatre Co. and The Triangle Youth Theatre. Productions tend to be alternative and socially aware but not be ready for the occasional mainstream item dropped in to boost the takings now and again. Community theatre play here, and it's also a good venue for dance and music. **Student Discount: is available.**

Royal Shakespeare Theatre + The Other Place + The Swan
Telephone: (0789) 295623
Stratford is but a mere hour away on coach or train, and you really should try and make the effort at least once whilst you're a student in Brum. Of course, the RST, is not the only place to see Shakespeare, but it's arguably the most provocative and the best. Aside from this main house, there is also **The Other Place** where you can find a mixed bag of contemporary and classic productions and the newly opened **Swan Theatre**, a Jacobean style play house, designed by noted architect Michael Reardon. Seating 430 people, it has a thrust stage surrounded on three sides by galleries and houses performances of the works of Shakespeare's notable contemporaries.

Midland Arts Centre
Cannon Hill Park. Telephone: 021-440 3838
Aside from offering some interesting 'alternative' theatre from touring and local companies, it also houses its much praised Cannon Hill Puppet Theatre for the young at heart. The Centre is a prime venue for visiting Dance Troupes. **Student Discount: is available.**

Crescent Theatre
Cumberland Street. Telephone: 021-643 5858
The Crescent is a self-financing amateur company with a professional out-look, and has established a good reputation for its wide ranging variety of plays including several premieres. An intimate theatre yet not so small as to be claustrophobic. The Crescent also offers an attractive auditorium, and a bar area. The Theatre normally stages between nine and ten productions a year ranging from light comedy to more experimental work.
Student Discount: On most shows.

The Old Rep
Station Street. Telephone: 021-783 0703
Amateur productions from its own and local companies form the staple of the fare on offer. The Old Rep has built a high reputation for fostering bright new talent.

E.S.G.B.

E.S.G.B.

Birmingham's theatre-land

The Birmingham Repertory Theatre

Freeman and Paul Henry. Ann Bradley remembers:

"I saw *First Impressions*. I had auditioned for a part in the show, but lost out to the late Mary Tamm. Years later in Stratford I bumped into the Musical Director, Stephen Hancock, and he very sweetly said that I had been his choice, but the director had the final say. The show had an excellent cast."

While the Rep was shifting its site, Birmingham's oldest music venue carried on regardless – at least until the 1990s. In the 1830s Joseph Aloysius Hansom had taken time out from inventing cabs to design the splendidly classical Town Hall. Still home to the City of Birmingham Symphony Orchestra in the 1970s, the Town Hall also hosted plenty of rock, blues and jazz concerts. The Town Hall website boasts that in its time it has staged shows

---

Andrew Harris' memories of a night in 1971 are especially vivid: well, it was his first gig, he did get bought a drink by a rock star

---

"from Count Basie to Black Sabbath". By the 1970s Basie's tours had tended to land at the New Street Odeon, but Black Sabbath certainly played the Town Hall often in the early 1970s.

The Sabs feature on Nigel Smith's list of bands he enjoyed at the Town Hall, alongside Magnum, Judas Priest, Sha Na Na, 10 Years After, Humble Pie, Budgie and the Sensational Alex Harvey Band. Likewise Chris Pitt's extended list puts Birmingham's heavy metal heroes alongside the likes of Pink Floyd, Jethro Tull, Captain Beefheart and – most memorably – "the incomparable, for me, Judee Sill on her one British tour." Regularly described as a "lost genius", Judee Sill died of a drug overdose in 1979. Canned Heat frequently appear on lists of favourite Town Hall concerts and for something a bit more out of the way Pete King found Frank Zappa "a blast".

Andrew Harris' memories of a night in 1971 are especially vivid: well, it was his first gig, he did get bought a drink by a rock star – and it was a pretty amazing bill:

"I went to my first gig with my brother and Dave Wakeling (The Beat and General Public) who was his best mate. Wakeling bought me a half of bitter. It was the 1971 Charisma tour at the Town Hall. Bottom of the bill was Genesis, then Lindisfarne. Top of the bill was Van Der Graff Generator."

April Phillips' best memory came in 1965, but it's too good not to mention: she actually held Bob Dylan's leather jacket while he did an encore.

Rather surprisingly militancy and social disruption came to the Town Hall not via rough rockers or leather-jacketed lefties, but from the longhairs of the CBSO. Growing unrest in the ranks even before 1970 grew until a dispute about the seating of a freelance viola player (yes, really!) led Music Director Louis Fremaux to exclaim, "The union wanted to manage

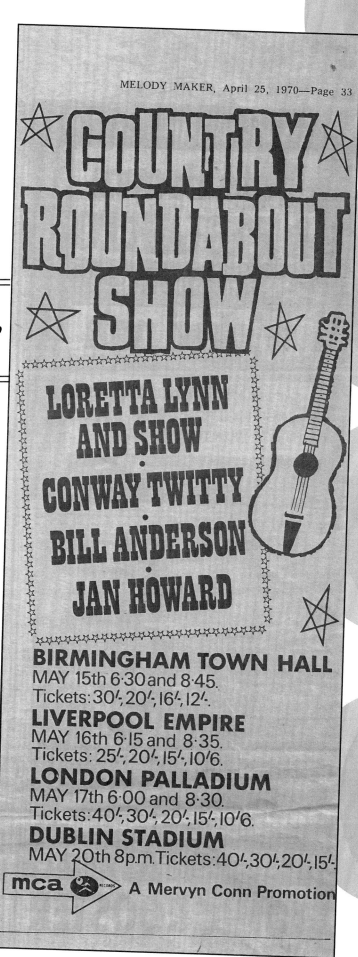

MELODY MAKER, April 25, 1970—Page 33

COUNTRY ROUNDABOUT SHOW

LORETTA LYNN AND SHOW
·
CONWAY TWITTY
·
BILL ANDERSON
·
JAN HOWARD

BIRMINGHAM TOWN HALL
MAY 15th 6·30 and 8·45.
Tickets: 30/-, 20/-, 16/-, 12/-.

LIVERPOOL EMPIRE
MAY 16th 6·15 and 8·35.
Tickets: 25/-, 20/-, 15/-, 10/6.

LONDON PALLADIUM
MAY 17th 6·00 and 8·30.
Tickets: 40/-, 30/-, 20/-, 15/-, 10/6.

DUBLIN STADIUM
MAY 20th 8 p.m. Tickets: 40/-, 30/-, 20/-, 15/-.

mca RECORDS A Mervyn Conn Promotion

the orchestra. Some of them wanted a revolution." Shortly afterwards he and the orchestra manager resigned. The spirit of Red Robbo flourished among the music stands!

Then there was the Odeon in New Street. Nick Shaw opined that the Town Hall was "a lead up to the Odeon – smaller and more intimate":

"I loved gigs at the Odeon – at times I don't know how they managed to show any films. The first gig I saw there was Emerson, Lake and Palmer. Both the Odeon and the Town Hall were killed off concert-wise by the NEC and the Indoor Arena."

Others found the larger venue less atmospheric, but Andrew Harris had a particular reason for preferring the Town Hall to the Odeon:

"The Odeon always had security which was pretty bad in attitude at times, but the best gig there was Bob Marley and the Wailers. The best at the Town Hall was John Cale – ex-Velvet Underground."

Paul Harris saw life at the Odeon from both sides ("My first gig was Kiss in 1976, then four years later I played there supporting UB40") and Gillon Jacoby proved lucky in his choice of friends:

"My friend Mark Culverwell who managed the Au Pairs and ran 021 Records always seemed to have a guest list wherever

---

It could be that at around 6 o'clock you might have seen Horace Panter and Jerry Dammers humping their gear into the pub

---

we went. I can remember great nights at the Odeon – King Creole and the Coconuts, Parliament, Funkadelic and the Brides of Funkenstein, Marvin Gaye, Chic, Sister Sledge..."

That's a nice eclectic mix, Gillon, but nothing compares with

the super-group that never was, conjured up by Jim Cronin's memories:

"I saw Meatloaf, Demis Roussos and Billy Connolly at the Odeon – but not on the same night!"

View from The Town Hall

If you had stood at the top of Hill Street sometime in the 1970s, with your back to The Town Hall and looked south, down the hill, on the corner of Swallow Street you would have seen the iconic pub The Golden Eagle with its great tradition of music.

It could be that at around 6 o'clock you might have seen Horace Panter and Jerry Dammers humping their gear into the pub, up that seemingly interminable staircase and onto the stage in the splendid gig room. That would have been The Specials who played a frequently sold-out residency there and, interestingly for a ska band, were often to be found supporting punk bands.

A little further down Hill Street, pretty much facing you on the intersection with Navigation Street, was Chetwyn's the tailor. Nothing remarkable about that, but the building

---

> ## By the 1970s the Cinephone's reputation had smoothed out a little and it was regarded by many as an arts cinema

---

had a great musical history even if it was fading by 1970. The first floor was occupied by the Laura Dixon School of Dance and at the weekends Laura let her hair down and was transformed into the Whisky-A-Gogo with capacity crowds for all-nighters with bands such as Georgie Fame and the Blue Flames, Alan Price and the Animals, Chris Farlowe and the Thunderbirds and Zoot Money's Big Roll Band. Sadly the Whisky closed in 1968, to be succeeded to diminishing effect by the Marquee and the Limelight Club.

Follow on down Hill Street to where Station Street goes off to the left, by the landmark iron-clad Victorian toilets, and you would have been confronted by The Crown Hotel. Originally designed to accommodate the circuit judges arriving at New Street Station, it later became the place where the UK's first live folk album was recorded, the site of a residency by the first Brum Beat group, The Modernaires, home to Henry's Blueshouse and, finally, in the late 1970s, the centre for Birmingham punk.

Panto time

Infant Dirty Stop Outs usually served their apprenticeship watching pantomimes and Birmingham for many years had the man known – much to his own displeasure – as "The King of Pantomime". Derek Salberg took over the Alexandra Theatre from his father in 1937 and devoted himself to the repertory company there (very much a thing of the past now) and the annual pantomime.

In 1977 Derek Salberg retired, but in 1979 the Alex was still offering a rare trio of comedians (Frankie Howerd, Bernard Bresslaw and Tommy Trinder) alongside the classic

Dame of Jack Tripp. With Les Dawson at the Hippodrome it must have been fun at the panto that year.

The Hippodrome's pantos in the seventies sometimes starred great clowns such as Norman Wisdom or comics steeped in the music hall such as Roy Hudd, but questions remain. What parts did they find for all three Bachelors? Why did they devote the 1977 panto to the stars of the television comedy, *Robin's Nest*? And how did Jim Davidson manage to tone down his material for the kiddies?

Vague or explicit?

Eyebrows were raised in 1962 when the Cinephone Continental Cinema, operated by Jacey Cinemas, who also owned the News Theatre and the Tatler in the city, opened on Bristol Street. It's true its grand opening had nothing seedy about it, all bowties and furs and the odd mayoral chain, with uniformed bobbies keeping back the eager crowds which featured a remarkable number of youngsters wagging it from school – the Pathe newsreel of the event is classic! For all that, in the eyes of the general public, it struggled for respectability.

By the 1970s the Cinephone's reputation had smoothed out a little and it was regarded by many as an arts cinema although films with such titles as *Diary of a Nudist, Summer with Monika* and *The Importance of Being Sexy* suggest otherwise.

The film programmes of the 1970s indicate a split personality. Certainly there were classics of the French nouvelle vague by the likes of Jean-Luc Godard and a film such as *Clochemerle* was the ideal fusion of Cinephone preoccupations: rude (a public lavvy, for Goodness' sake!), French and based on a novel of some repute. But much of the time was taken up by such uncompromising treats as *Erotic Fantasies*. Carol Maye, not, we suspect, a regular at the Cinephone, didn't let on what film she watched, but summed up the audience neatly:

"I saw a 3D affair with my 18-year-old best friend and a smattering of men in macs and hats."

Matthew Edwards saw a fine double bill in the 1970s, *Performance* and *Easy Rider,* but 40-odd years later is still grumbling, "Both terrible quality prints!".

It was all very continental: of course it was an acknowledged fact in the 1970s that Europe was the source of everything erotic and most things arty! So the cinema boasted fauteuils de luxe and a Continental Coffee Lounge operated by none other than Andre Drucker.

Drucker had escaped from Nazi Austria and made Birmingham his home. In 1958 he opened his first continental coffee lounge – the later to be famous La Boheme in Aston Street – but it wasn't until he opened a bakery in Moseley and recruited a master baker from Hamelin in Germany that the Drucker cake revolution took off. It's wryly reported that Birmingham folk were at first shocked that something called Schwarzwalderkirschtorte cost as much as six iced buns, but ultimately Andre Drucker was one of the people who helped the British public to eat Black Forest gateau without the aid of a dictionary!

The Boomtown Rats in action in Birmingham

BRUM FOLK SEPT 6-8 74

Alex Atterson
Harvey Andrews/
Graham Cooper
Stan Arnold
Derek Brimstone
Boys of the Lough
Tony Capstick
Jasper Carrott
Peter & Chris Coe
Coventry Mummers
Cosmatheka
Shirley Collins
Decameron

Barbara Dickson
Earlsdon Morris
Etchingham Steam Band
Free Reed
Gasworks
John James
Matthews Brothers
Pigsty Hill Light Orch
Liverpool Poets —
Roger McGough/
Brian Patten/
Adrian Henri
Jon Raven

Mike Raven & Joan Mills
Hugh Rippon
Barry Roberts
Dave Start
Sour Grapes
Jake Thackray
Timms Punch & Judy
Therapy
The Watersons
Webbs Wonders
White Hart Morris

Concerts, stalls, work-
shops, films, morris
sides, mumming, late-
nights, singalongs and
four bars at the
Birmingham Repertory
Theatre,
Broad Street
Birmingham B1 2EP
Box Office: 021-236-4455
Enquiries: Roger
Lancaster 021-236-6711

CITY OF BIRMINGHAM SYMPHONY ORCHESTRA

SEASON 1974-75

Highlights include:

SIR ADRIAN BOULT
KYUNG-WHA CHUNG
DAVID OISTRAKH
LES PERCUSSIONS DE STRASBOURG
HANS RICHTER-HAASER
RUGGIERO RICCI
NARCISO YEPES

JUBILEE OF HIS FIRST CBSO CONCERT
BEETHOVEN VIOLIN CONCERTO
PROKOFIEV VIOLIN CONCERTO 1
CAGE/BIRTWISTLE/XENAKIS
THE BEETHOVEN PIANO CONCERTOS
TCHAIKOVSKY VIOLIN CONCERTO
RODRIGO GUITAR CONCERTO

Singers aged 18/45 are invited to audition for the CBSO CHORUS, whom LOUIS FRÉMAUX will be conducting in the Requiems of Berlioz, Fauré and Verdi and in major choral works by Beethoven, Mahler and Ravel. Telephone 021-236 1555 for application form.

Annual Prospectus
on sale 25p + 7p postage from
THE BOX OFFICE, TOWN HALL, BIRMINGHAM, B3 3DQ

Chapter 10
Jasper, Laurie and Meg

At the dawn of the 1970s fans of folk music and comedy would make their way every Monday evening to The Boggery Folk Club in The Bank House, Knowle, to be entertained by Jasper Carrott, Malcolm Stent and their guests. On one particularly memorable occasion the famed French violinist Stephane Grappelli was joined onstage by a 12-year-old kid, one Nigel Kennedy!

The Boggery saw a break with the more earnest style of 1960s folk. In place of the traditional and the political, Jasper Carrott put irreverence on the agenda. In the 1970s The Boggery relocated to two different Solihull venues, The Old Moseleians Club and then the Malt Shovel. Along the way Jasper Carrott's career blossomed. He became The Boggery's main attraction, released his first album, *Jasper Carrott in the Club*, depicting an apparently heavily pregnant

Jasper Carrott and Bev Bevan

Along the way Jasper Carrott's career blossomed. He became The Boggery's main attraction

---

Jasper outside Mothercare, and had a big chart hit in 1975, with *Funky Moped* backed with *Magic Roundabout*. In 1978 he landed his hugely successful London Weekend Television show *An Audience with Jasper Carrott*. Jasper devoted as much time as he was able to The Boggery, but stardom beckoned and by the end of the decade he was well on the way to world domination. The club survived to the mid-eighties.

Jasper Carrott remembers:
"The Boggery started in February 1969. I left in about 1974 or '75 because there was a lot of work thanks to the single and the album. The single got into the Top Five and I didn't have time to concentrate on The Boggery. Then in 1978 I had the television series, *An Audience with Jasper Carrott*. Malcolm Stent used to run the club from then and Les Ward who opened it with me continued for about 16 years. I was always welcome and went back, though doing folk clubs when you could fill a 5000 seater was a bit silly really.

"In the early days I did a lot of football material. I was obviously very interested in it and folk clubs were for working class people and they watch football. I did a very famous routine about Birmingham City playing Manchester United. That would have been 1976 and it was the first

game of the season at Old Trafford. I had flown in from the Isle of Man and met up with half a dozen mates and we got seats in the stand. It was in the days when Manchester United was a very dangerous ground for visiting supporters. We had a friend who wasn't that into football but liked the camaraderie. All the Birmingham City supporters were in the same block and, no matter what we said, our friend would stand up and shout, 'Go on Blues, shove it up 'em!' There were lines of people ready to punch his face. There was a very famous line that came out of it, because he had gone to the canteen and was at a long bar and he saw me and shouted, 'Carrott! They've got no cowing Bovril!' I did the whole sketch off the top of my head once in Manchester because I was struggling because they all knew the material. It became a very popular routine.

EVENTS

FRIDAY 29 NOVEMBER
FACES: Odeon, New St (R)
EDGAR BROUGHTON BAND: JB's (R)
SUNDANCE, O, SHEERWATER, JASPER CARROT,
CARTOONS, ROCK FILMS, DISCO, CHEAP REC-
ORDS. The Xmas Party at B'ham Univ (R)
DRUID: Aston Univ (R)
WIZZ JONES: Brum Studio (F)
TERRY McCANN: Bell & Pump (F)
SINGERS NIGHT: Old Crown (F)
Unconfirmed: Unicorn (F)
SCOTCH MIST: Matlock College, Derbys (F)
KEN INGRAMS ORPHEANS: Shantasea (J)
RAY CONNIF SINGERS + ORCH: Town Hall (J?)
CARMINA BURANA by CARL ORFF: Full danced
version. Singers: Robert Bateman, Sandra
Dugdale, Bonaventura Bottone, Univ Music
Society Choir. Choreographer, Jane Wine-
arls. Setting of mediaval poems about
love, death & fate. Inaugral event of
B'ham University Centenary Celebrations.
Great Hall, B'ham University. 7.30.
Tickets £1.20, £1.60, students 60p.

Saturdays

EVERY SATURDAY:
THREE HEADED DOG: Railway (R)
DISCO: B'ham Univ Union (R)
MIKE MILLER BAND + DISCO: Locarno (R)
STEVE GIBBONS BAND: Incognito, lunchtime(R)
EAGLE JAZZBAND: Old Crown (J)
ANDREWS PRIDDEY DUNN + SMITH & JONES:
 Opposite Lock (J)
PRITCHARD NICHOLLS DEGVILLE + CHUMS:
 Crown Brownhills, Free (J)
SARATOGA JAZZBAND + GUESTS: Waterworks (J)
MOULIN ROUGE: Royal Exchange (J)
TOMMY BURTON + SPORTING HOUSE QUINTET:
 Shrewsbury Arms (J)
FRANK MILDEN TRIO + COMEDIANS: Lord Raglan
JAZZ & SWING: Selly Park Tavern (J)
RESIDENTS & GUESTS: Brewood & Fletch (F)

SATURDAY 26 OCTOBER
CHRIS STANTON'S TUNDRA: JB's (R)

LINDISFARNE: Town Hall (R)
HUDSON FORD: Leicester Univ (R)
FREEFALL: Bogarts (J/R)
RAYMOND FROGGATT: Barbarellas (R)
MARISA PABLOS (Harp) & CHRIS HYDE-WHITE
(Flute): Art Gallery 7.30. CBSO members (C)
THE FLYING DUTCHMAN: Welsh National Opera,
Hippodrome 7.30 (C)
DEREK & DOROTHY ELLIOT: Gothic (F)
STAR: Closed for private function
THE VILLAGE MINSTREL: Poetry & Folk music
from the work of John Clare. Alumwell
School Walsall 7.30 (F)
MIKE JAMES & BARRIE ROBERTS: Songsmiths
CHRISTIE HENNESSY: Brewood (F)
WHITE ON BLACK: Fletch (F)

SATURDAY 2 NOVEMBER
STEVE GIBBONS BAND: Loughborough Coll (R)
SORAHAN: High Hall, Brum Univ (R)
BE BOP DELUXE: JB's (R)
GONZALEZ: Barbarella's (R)
BASIC TRUTH: Rebbecca's (R)
ELGAR: CBSO Worcester Cathedral 7.30 (C)
SIMON BOCCANEGRA: Welsh Nat Opera,
Hippodrome, 7.30 (C)
ST MICHAELS SINGERS, ORCH DA CAMERA,
ALAN CIVIL: Mozart, Coventry Cathedral
7.45 (C)
LES SYLPHIDES: Royal Ballet, Grand
Theatre, Wolves 2.30/7.30 (C)
SINGERS NIGHT: Gothic (F)
BOB BUCKLE: Brewood (F)
ALEX CAMPBELL: Songsmith's (F)
PATCHWORK FOLK: Star (F)

SATURDAY 9 NOVEMBER
FLUFF: Newman College (R)
To be booked: JB's (R)
LIMMIE + FAMILY COOKING: Barbarella's (R)
ALBERT HERRING: English Opera Group,
Grand Theatre, Wolverhampton 7.30 (C)
NEW BUDAPEST QUARTET: Haydn, Brahms, Bar
tok. B'ham Chamber Music Soc, Art Gallery
Tickets £1.25 at door or from Town Hall
Box Office. Students 50p in adv from 16,

York Rd B16 9JB
ENGLISH CHAMBER ORCHESTRA: Brandenburg
Concertos 3,4,5. B'ham Bach Society,
B'ham Cathedral 7.30. (C)
MIDLAND YOUTH ORCHESTRA & MARGARET WHARAM
CHOIR: Brahms, Bach, Mendelssohn, Perry.
Town Hall 7.30. Cheap (C)
EKKEHARD SCHNEKE: International Organ
Recital.Coventry Cathedral 7.45. (C)
ALLEGRI STRING QUARTET,YEHUDI MENUHIN,
HEPHZIBAH MENUHIN: Elgar 40th Anniversary
Worcester Cathedral 7.30pm. (C)

SATURDAY 16 NOVEMBER
JACK THE LAD: JB's (R)
QUEEN + HUSTLER: Town Hall (R)
DETROIT EMERALDS: Barbarella's (R)
JOHN CHAPMAN + BIDFORD BAND: Bidford
Dance (R)
SINGERS NIGHT: Gothic (F)
BARRIE ROBERTS + MICK JAMES: Songsmith's
Star: closed
SCOTCH MIST: Brewood (F)

SATURDAY 23 NOVEMBER
A BAND CALLED 'O': JB's (R)
THE TIMES: Barbarella's (R)
LISCARROL: Gothic (F)
ALISTAIR ANDERSON: Songsmith's (F)
PETE DOUGLAS: Star (F)
SCOTCH MIST: Fletch (F)
LONDON FESTIVAL BALLET: ETUDE PRODIGAL
SON IN RAGTIME Birmingham Hippodrome
7.30 (C)
CBSO & CHOIR, ROY MASSEY(Organ): Dvorak's
Te Deum, Town Hall 7.30 (C)

SATURDAY 30 NOVEMBER
FACES: Odeon (R)
STEVE GIBBONS: Trent Poly (R)
HYKELLS: Greenlands Social Club, Long-
bridge Lane B31 (R)
CASABLANCA: JB's (R)
SINGERS NIGHT: Gothic (F)
BARRIE ROBERTS & MIKE JAMES: Songsmith's

"I did a song called *Aston Villa Skinhead Supporters Club Song*. That's where the line 'You'll Never Walk Again' came from and they showed it on television.

"After the hit single in 1975, I did a week at The Old Rep in Station Street. I did the Town Hall and after 1978 I was regularly at The Hippodrome and I would do a week there every three years. I was very big in those days. I did 125 concerts and 124 were total sell outs, and the only one that didn't sell out was Burnley because I thought Burnley came under Yorkshire television, but it actually came under Granada who hadn't shown the series *An Audience with Jasper Carrott*.

"The way television eats up material is frightening. When I did a 40 minute show for BBC on a Saturday night live, *Carrott's Lib*, I worked out there were over 700 man hours of writing, just to try and get the material that would be good and funny. Writing in comedy is everything, performing is the easy bit. If you've got the material, it's easy, but, if you haven't got the material, you're struggling. But it's part and parcel. If it was easy there'd be thousands. If you look back to 1978 comedy was really 10 minutes on the Cilla Black show, and then when I did *Audience with Jasper Carrott* people started to realise what I call conversational comedy. Myself, Billy Connolly and Max Boyce changed the face of comedy."

In the 1950s and 1960s traditional jazz gained a never-to-be-repeated popularity, with jazz bands hitting the charts

In the 1950s and 1960s traditional jazz gained a never-to-be-repeated popularity, with jazz bands hitting the charts and getting bookings at such places as The London Palladium. Each major city tended to have its flagship band, often with a local reference in its name: Merseysippi Jazz Band from Liverpool, for instance, or The Clyde Valley Stompers from Glasgow – or The Second City Jazzmen.

The band had a national reputation, with other top bands – Kenny Ball or Chris Barber maybe – coming to play at the Midland Jazz Club in Digbeth where the Second City had a residency from 1956 to 1972 in the same room where the Ian Campbell Folk Club held sway. By the 1970s jazz was falling down Dirty Stop Outs' lists of priorities, but there was still plenty to be heard around Birmingham.

Terry McGrath of the Eureka Jazz Band offers a thumb-nail sketch of the Birmingham traditional jazz scene in the 1970s. The bands, he claims, were divided into three separate camps, but the musicians in any camp were all "young, keen, self-taught and narrow-minded about their particular style."

Old-style jazz from Norman Field's Nighthawk Orchestra

Judging from the sleeve notes (which incidently are very good), Harper takes this piece particularly seriously himself, and with due cause, for he has succeeded in saying almost everything that he has been trying to say for the past five years since he started recording. It is a celebration, and the album is a celebration of his return. We can only hope that the physical pressures of singing do not eventually beat him, and that he will continue to produce records of equally high musical quality, and without compromising his principals.

(Owing to a shortage of space, some 'pop' reviews and photos have been omitted and will appear in the next issue. Apologies to all concerned.-Ed)

Thursday 1.
BAREFOOT & MAGNUM, resident at the Rum Runner.
BIG JUMP BAND at Rebeccas for 3 nights.
A band from long ago - THE PLATTERS - at Barbarellas for three nights.
PEARLY KINGS at the Lafayette.

Friday 2.
Disco at the Stone Manor (+ every Friday).

Saturday 3.
CARNIVAL at the Lafayette.
Disco at the Belfry (+ every saturday).

Sunday 4.
DES O'CONNOR at New Cresta for one week.
FLIRTATIONS at La Dolce Vita for one week.
'Make It Motown' Disco at the Top Rank.
SHOW BANDITS at the Lafayette.

Monday 5.
Disco at the Belfry (+ every Monday)
BUDDY GRECO at Barbarellas for one week.

Tuesday 6.
Disco at Stone Manor (+ every Tuesday)
FROGMORE at the Chalet Country Club, Rednal.
FLIRTATIONS at Bloomers, Tivoli Centre, Yardley.
JOHN LEES DISCO SHOW at the Top Rank (ev. Tues)

Thursday 8.
SMILING HARD at Rebeccas for three nights.
SHOW BANDITS at the Chalet.

Friday 9.
PERCY SLEDGE makes a very welcome return, for one night only at Barbarellas.

Sunday 11.
OUR WAY OF LIFE at the Lafayette, Wolverhampton.

Monday 12.
PAGAN CHORUS at Rebeccas for one week.
DRAGONS PLAYGROUND at Barbarellas for 1 week.

Tuesday 13.
PERCY SLEDGE at the Lafayette, Wolverhampton.
GUINEVERE at the Chalet Country Club.

Thursday 15.
JIMMY RUFFIN at Barbarellas for 3 nights.
MUTTON CHOP BANJO BAND at the Chalet.

Sunday 18.
MICHAEL BENTINE at the New Cresta for one week.
BLACKWATER JUNCTION at La Dolce Vita " ".
NORTH STARS at the Lafayette.

Tuesday 20.
SCREAMING LORD SUTCH at Bloomers (+ Th. & Fr)
TINTINO MAX at the Chalet.

Thursday 22.
The O'JAYS at Barbarellas for 3 nights.
SALVATION at the Lafayette.
SIGHT AND SOUND at the Chalet.

Sunday 25.
CRESTAS at the Lafayette.

Monday 26.
FAIRGROUND at Rebeccas for one week.
COASTERS at Barbarellas " " ".
Ex boppers reunion with the TREMELOES at the La Dolce Vita.

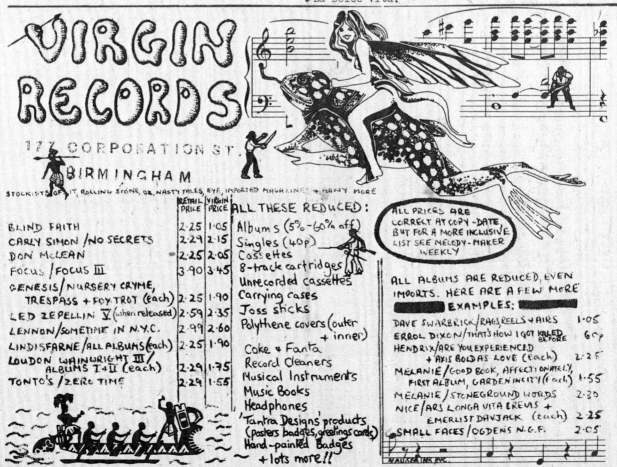

In the New Orleans camp were Danny Pawson and the Artesian Hall Stompers and Ken Pye's Creole Serenaders, claiming to play the black N'Awlins style with no compromise and commanding a small, but devoted, following. The second camp, according to Terry, and the most saleable, were the followers of Barber, Bilk and Ball, with slick arrangements and matching outfits. This well-rehearsed group included the Zenith Hot Stompers and George Huxley's Band besides the Second City. Finally Terry defined the comedy entertainers as providing barn-storming jazz, totally irreverent and politically incorrect, with (literally) bells and whistles. The Eagle and Northside Jazz Bands headed this camp.

The Eagle Jazz Band was sufficiently in the entertainment mainstream to audition for *New Faces*, ATV's answer to *Opportunity Knocks*, in 1974. They didn't win, but made a great impression on the performer who did, a Birmingham University student called Victoria Wood. She became a fan of the band, attending their gigs at the Golden Eagle and the Old Crown at Digbeth, even acting as intermission pianist sometimes!

Recording studios and record shops

Situated on a car park at the back of Ladbrooke's, the splendid piano emporium, and dating from the late 1960s, was a small – shall we say cramped? – recording studio. Zella Studio was owned and sound engineered by an escaped schoolteacher Johnny Haynes and named, apparently, after

a former girlfriend. Unimpressive it may have been, when viewed from outside, but it was in fact the go-to recording facility for most of the leading Birmingham rock, reggae and pop bands. The equipment was basic, the facilities minimal, but Johnny was able to get a good and exciting sound which actually is about all anyone could ask for in a recording studio.

In between working as a jobbing producer on discs by everyone from school choirs and cinema organists, Johnny Haynes engineered the first recording by Black Sabbath and worked with such groups as Locomotive, the Spencer Davis Group, the Move, the Uglys, Idle Race, Magnum, Bashara and Band of Joy – quite a list!

1970s Birmingham could boast various iconic record stores: the impressive new Virgin Records on Bull Street, managed by the irrepressible Phil Middleton, the musicians' social club on Cannon Street that was Reddington's Rare Records, the Diskery, Hurst Street's home to jazz records, and, tucked away in the Gun Quarter's Loveday Street, the modestly named Record and Tape Centre.

This was nirvana to the jazz collector many of whom made the pilgrimage to Ray Purslow's treasure house from miles away, to be greeted by the words writ large across a beam facing the entrance: "If you have anything bad to say about Francis Albert Sinatra. Do not say it in here." (After all, Purslow ran the UK branch of the Frank Sinatra Fan Club).

From that it may be deduced that there was a certain degree of intolerance operating in the Record and Tape Centre.

Terry McGrath and friends

If you want proof, how about this? Overheard encounter between a somewhat naïve customer and the formidable Mr. Purslow:

Clearly impressed customer:
"What a terrific specialist shop you have here!"
Mr. P. (suspiciously): "What do you mean, specialist?"
Customer (stuttering): "Er, jazz specialist, I mean...er..."
Mr. P. (delivering his punch-line with aplomb): "We're not jazz specialists. We specialise in small group swing from 1948 to 1952." Collapse of well-meaning customer.

Even Stop Outs stopped in...

...to watch *Crossroads*, the flagship programme of ATV, Birmingham's independent television franchise. *Crossroads*, the soap set in a motel in a village near to Birmingham, could be said to have divided opinion.

In those days regional independent television operated more independently and it took eight years from its first showing to become fully networked, Granada finally falling into line in 1972. If that was a bit sniffy, what about Lady Plowden's remark in 1979 in an IBA report that it was "distressingly popular"? Or for that matter Victoria Wood's instantly recognisable spoof, *Acorn Antiques*, all wobbly scenery, missed entries and fluffed lines?

So it was bad? Not in the opinion of the 15 million viewers who from time to time toppled *Coronation Street* from the most-watched spot in the mid-1970s or the *TV Times* readers who voted Noelle Gordon, the motel's chatelaine Meg Richardson, the Most Popular Female Personality with monotonous regularity.

And what could the BBC put up against Magic Meg? How about Princess Anne? Her Royal Highness opened the *Pebble Mill* complex in leafy Edgbaston on June 10th, 1971, the BBC's home for over 30 years and the site of one of the iconic programmes of daytime television, newly restriction-free, *Pebble Mill at One*.

Laurie at the Lychee Garden

In the 1970s Birmingham's now flourishing Chinatown did not exist. The oft-told story of how the Chung Ying Restaurant was set up in a former synagogue and gradually other businesses clustered around it dates from 1981. But that is not to say there were no Chinese restaurants in the city. Possibly the first (and certainly one of the best), the Lychee Garden in Edgbaston, dates back to 1969 and one night in the late 1970s was the setting for an incident that, depending on your point of view was either funny or an object lesson in the mindlessness of racial prejudice – or both!

At that time one of the few things that fans of Birmingham City, Aston Villa and West Bromwich Albion could agree on was that The Three Degrees (footballing version) were something special. At that time the Albion's ground-breaking trio of black footballers, Laurie Cunningham, Cyrille Regis and Brendan Batson, were key elements in a team that played wonderfully exciting football and all but swept all before them in the 1978-79 season.

One evening Laurie and his white girlfriend, having just enjoyed their meal at the Lychee Garden, stepped outside and had hardly gone 60 paces before three white youths started shouting racial insults and, somewhat rashly, set about giving Laurie a good thrashing. In a flash Laurie floored two of the thugs. The third ran away into the night, followed by one of his mates who had hauled himself up off the pavement, leaving their chum on his back with Laurie standing over him, awaiting his next move.

Suddenly it dawned on the youth. With a fan's excitement, he shouted, 'You're Laurie Cunningham!'. It didn't actually end with handshakes all round, nor did the would-be assailant ask for Laurie's autograph or get presented with free tickets for the next Albion match, but he did scuttle away into the night with a fine story to tell.

Jazz on the march, The Eureka Brass Band

Chapter 11
Startime at the Hawthorns

Unlike today, 1970s football was not part of show business – unless, that is, you happened to support West Bromwich Albion! Manager Ron Atkinson cannily combined talent spotting and pioneering social attitudes by signing up The Three Degrees – not the hit-making Philadelphia vocal group, but a trio of outstanding black players! At a time when one black player in a team was a novelty (and the object of racist chants, hurled bananas, and monkey noises) Big Ron boldly signed Laurie Cunningham, Cyrille Regis and Brendan Batson.

Though Regis and Batson had fairly long careers at the Albion, the three were together for one season only – 1978-79 – and in that season the Albion were flying, capable of beating any team in the First Division. Ignoring racial abuse, Cunningham, Regis and Batson did what they did best, produce magnificent football.

The highlight of the season came on December 30th, 1978, Manchester United versus West Bromwich Albion, with the Baggies winning 5-3

The highlight of the season came on December 30th, 1978, Manchester United versus West Bromwich Albion, with the Baggies winning 5-3 in what was described as "The Game of the Century". The Three Degrees, as christened by Big Ron – or possibly his publicist – were central to that victory at a cold and snowy Old Trafford, with Regis and Cunningham both scoring. The Albion finished third that season, chasing Liverpool and Everton and qualifying for Europe.

Unfortunately, by the time the Albion's European campaign began and ended with defeat by Carl Zeiss Jena in Autumn 1979, Laurie Cunningham was no longer with the club. He had signed for Real Madrid in the summer, going on to a nomadic career in Europe before being killed in a high-speed car crash near Madrid in 1989. In 1979 he gained a full England cap, only a year after Viv Anderson had become the first black player to get that distinction. The late Cyrille Regis went on to star for all the top teams in the region and pick up five England caps and Brendan Batson became a distinguished football administrator, but all three are best remembered for The Season of the Three Degrees. And in 2015 the memory was kept alive by a triple statue in the centre of West Bromwich.

Sheila, Helen and Valerie are The Three Degrees.

Brendon, Laurie and Cyrille are also The Three Degrees.

Good luck from

The Three Degrees

The Three Degrees current hit album 'New Dimensions' produced by Giorgio Moroder, featuring the 3 hit singles 'The Runner', 'Woman in Love' and 'Giving up Giving in'.

The Three Degrees in a West Bromwich Albion programme from 1979

Though technically a Black Country club, the Albion, based only a couple of miles outside the city limits, can boast a big following in Birmingham, but Aston Villa and Birmingham City are genuine big city rivals. For the Blues, the 1970s was the Age of Trevor Francis who spent the decade gradually changing from teenage prodigy to Britain's first million pound footballer – and in 1979 the club acquired a celebrity director, Jasper Carrott, who shares his memories of the club in the seventies:

"Birmingham City had always been a side that were not good enough for the First Division but too good for the Second and they bounced up and down. In 1972 we went to Leyton Orient and if we won we would go up to the First Division. If we didn't then Millwall would go up. On the night Millwall brought about 5000 fans to encourage Leyton Orient. It was a magical night. We got there before the ground was open! Birmingham City fans were so vocal. There was a bomb scare. We all had to get onto the pitch whilst they were sorting it out and the bloke was saying, 'Get on the bloody pitch, there's a bomb.' Anyway we won 1-0. Of course Trevor Francis was playing then. There was the very famous game when he made an appearance when we played Bolton Wanderers at St. Andrews where he scored 4 goals when he was 16 years old. He took this free kick and every time I talk to Trevor about it he adds on a couple of yards. I think it's about a 200 yard free kick at the moment. It was just a magical night and he became an overnight sensation."

In 1976 Jasper became the first individual to sponsor a First Division game:

"I'd released an album called Jasper *Carrott Rabbits On And On And On...*, and with the backing of the record company I was the first ever individual to sponsor a game. It was between Birmingham City and Sunderland. A guy who owned

> **"I became a director in 1979. Jim Smith had just taken over, sold Trevor Francis and bought almost half a team with the money..."**

a car showroom and was a big Birmingham fan offered to supply the scorer of the sixth goal against any team with a Triumph TR6 sports car. Birmingham had been away to Derby County and had beaten them 5-1, but nobody got a sixth goal. It was only a couple weeks prior to the game against Sunderland, so at half time we had six Derby County players on cardboard stuck into the ground and I came out with my Birmingham City kit and I dribbled round all the players that were staked into the ground. I got to the final

one and then he tripped me up and I took the penalty and scored, therefore winning the sixth goal and supposedly getting the car and then two men in white coats ran onto the pitch and escorted me off. It was just a stupid stunt, but the crowd loved it. It was great entertainment and it was the story of 1976.

"I became a director in 1979. Jim Smith had just taken over, sold Trevor Francis and bought almost half a team with the money. I was there for just under three years and I left in '82 when they brought in the Aston Villa manager Ron Saunders, much against my advice, and I left under protest because I made an agreement with the directors that any deal involving Birmingham City over 10 million pounds had to be ratified by the whole board and they went against that. In a way, I'll be honest, it was my way of getting out.

"We got to three semi-finals in the FA Cup – and lost every time. The closest was when we played Fulham and we drew at Sheffield, 1-1. I think. The replay was at Manchester City at Maine Road and it went to extra time. There were seconds left and it was still 0-0. We were talking about the replay at Highbury when suddenly the ball went to Birmingham City's goalkeeper. The ball bounced off his chest and this Fulham player couldn't believe his luck, stuck it in the net and Fulham won 1-0. Everybody that was there who was a Birmingham City fan remembers it. Fulham were in the Second Division and we were in the First and we were micro-seconds away

Gary Newbon and Jasper Carrott meet two of the Three Degrees

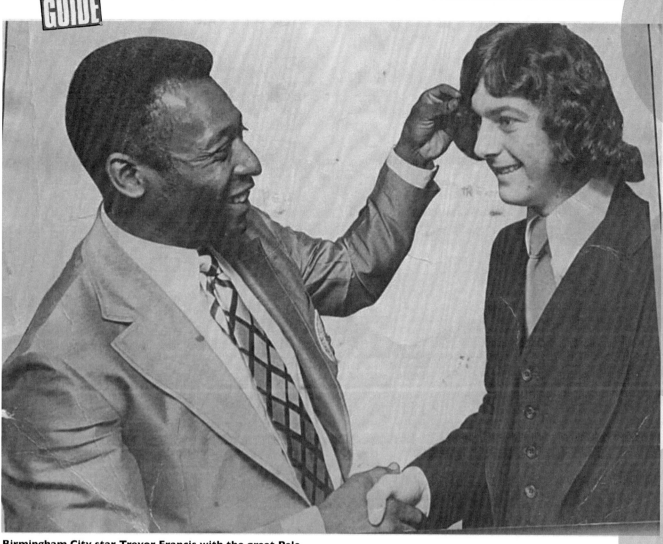

Birmingham City star Trevor Francis with the great Pele

from a Wembley appearance. Many years later, I was playing golf in Spain in a celebrity thing with a golf commentator, can't remember his name, but we were the celebs. I was playing with someone I knew and he was playing with someone he knew. We went down the first tee and he said, 'I'm Peter Mitchell.' It was the guy that scored the goal that took Fulham to Wembley. I spent the next 17 holes trying to hit the bastard with a golf ball, but I'm not very good at golf."

The Villa in the 1970s maybe lacked the glamour of pop star fame and million pound transfers – and, let's face it, manager Ron Saunders was not a man to have much time for glamour – but it was the Villa who won two League Cups in the 1970s and went on to conquer Europe a few years later.

Dave Woodhall offers a claret-and-blue-eyed version of the 1970s:

"Purists might insist that the seventies began on New Year's Day 1971, but Villa fans will tell you that the decade, if not modern football, started a few days earlier, December 21st, 1970, when Third Division Aston Villa took on the might of Manchester United, Charlton, Best, Law et al, in a League Cup semi-final second leg. The first leg, at Old Trafford, had ended in a 1-1 draw with both teams convinced that they were on their way to Wembley, United because the opposition were merely a Third Division stepping stone, Villa because, well, because they were Aston Villa. Roared on by over 60,000 frenzied supporters, Villa recovered from going

a goal down to run out 3-2 winners on aggregate. Everything that followed in that memorable decade could be traced back to the incredible, emotional night when the original Biggest Club in the World rose from its slumbers.

"The following years saw Pele appearing at Villa Park, record crowds, promotion, Ron Saunders, another

---

"The following years saw Pele appearing at Villa Park, record crowds, promotion, Ron Saunders, another promotion and the League Cup..."

---

promotion and the League Cup. There was Andy Gray, the first player in Birmingham to be equally at home on the front pages as in the sports headlines, who once scored a hat-trick, then went off early to attend the opening of his night club, the Holy City Zoo on Livery Street. Liverpool were destroyed 5-1 in their first European Cup season, there was another League Cup where Chris Nicholl scored with a howitzer that witnesses swear came from the car park and Brian Little, whose name still causes middle-aged men to grown misty-eyed, got the winner in the last of 330 minutes of a three-game final. Johan Cruyff played for Barcelona in Villa Park's first great European night.

"Saunders fell out first with John Gidman, who had made the position of full-back fashionable, then Gray and former chairman Doug Ellis and naturally had the beating of them all on his way to putting together the most successful team the city has ever seen. At the beginning of the seventies the recently sacked Tommy Docherty had said, 'Aston Villa will play in the European Cup one day.' As the decade ended, nobody could have known how close his words were to coming true."

Extra Time at Lorenzo's

If Blues and Baggies fans could claim to be bitter rivals, the same could not be said for their managers in the 1970s. Ron Atkinson and his Blues counterpart Jim Smith were regularly to be found eating and drinking together on Friday evenings at the famed Park Street restaurant of man-about-football Lorenzo Ferrari. Inevitably, as the evening wore on, footballistas would gather in the bar and talk football – what else? As the banter developed, Big Ron would always cause a stir by saying, "Come on, Jim, tell me, how much do you want for Trevor?"

In the end, of course, it was another of football's larger than life characters, Brian Clough, who lured Trevor Francis away from St. Andrew's.

And there is a sort of follow-up to all this. In 1979, when Big Ron and the management of Real Madrid came to terms over the transfer of Laurie Cunningham, the deal was signed at Lorenzo's.

Gary Newbon was there right from the start:

"Lorenzo opened his restaurant in December 1971 when he moved up from London in the same month that I moved to Birmingham to be ATV's new sports presenter.

"Lorenzo's sparkling personality drew a cross-section of people including Cliff Richard, Barry Manilow, stars of screen and theatre, the pantomime big names, top sports people, TV presenters, etc.

"I formed the Midlands Soccer Writers Association which staged bi-monthly luncheons with a range of big-name football speakers: Bill Shankly, Brian Clough, Don Revie, Trevor Francis, the Derby County League champions under

> ## "The following years saw Pele appearing at Villa Park, record crowds, promotion, Ron Saunders, another promotion and the League Cup..."

ATV's Gary Newbon with Kevin Keegan

Dave Mackay with the trophy, Johan Cruyff when Barcelona played at Villa Park, Jasper Carrott and so on."

Jasper Carrott, who incidentally wrote a football column for the *Sports Argus*, adds his memories of Lorenzo's:

"Lorenzo's was the headquarters of the Midlands Soccer Writers. I remember there was one classic meeting when we had the minister for drought, it was Dennis Howell. It had been pissing down for three weeks and I remember I introduced him and said, "When's it gonna stop, this bloody rain?", which brought the place down and I got a admonishment from Dennis, but it was all funny.

"There was a famous trip to Italy when Birmingham played in Rome at a big stadium and the contingent went out from Birmingham airport and I think we lost 2-1. Lorenzo had taken so much stick about being Italian in Birmingham over all the years and as soon as the plane touched the ground he stood up at the front of the plane and said, 'You bleeding foreigners, get out of my fucking country!' We went along to the game and tried to get into our seats, but it was just jammed solid and every seat had two people in it, it was absolute mayhem. There was tear gas coming across the grounds, everybody's eyes were streaming. Billy Wright was sitting on the lap of somebody else and they were saying, 'This is Billy Wright. He played for England.' About five Italians got up and made him a place to sit because it was Billy Wright and because the Italians know a lot about football. Things went on that I can't relate. Lorenzo had arranged some bizarre things, bizarre restaurants, bizarre drinks and bizarre entertainers. It was a very famous trip."

Back to Gary Newbon:

"On August 23rd 1972 I proposed to my wife (on her birthday) in there through Lorenzo. I was in Munich at the time covering the Olympic Games for ITV and I rang from there to get a yes. I just left the ring with Lorenzo. The restaurant was packed and the waiters brought out cake, flowers and champagne. I had my stag party there the night before my wedding and after the reception my family all went there for dinner with us before we went off on honeymoon!"

Sadly Lorenzo's as a restaurant stayed open for only a matter of months after the return of Signor Ferrari to Italy where he, in turn, found the Mafia a much more troublesome proposition than the good folk of Birmingham had ever been.

Grandstanding!

Ron Atkinson's ability to use publicity even brought The Three Degrees Detroit-style to the Hawthorns for a photo-op, but he had nothing to do with the appearance of The Baggies on record. Birmingham label, Grandstand Records, carried away by the wave of euphoria, celebrated by bringing out a blue and white 45 rpm vinyl record imaginatively titled *West Bromwich Albion*.

Suitably Caribbean, in calypso style, complete with steel drums, *West Bromwich Albion* was sung by Ray King, ironically a Coventry City supporter, and featured a photograph of a flying Cyrille Regis on the label. For pure poetry what could be better than this?

"There's shooting stars down West Bromwich way
At the Hawthorns on Saturday,
Strolling around the opposing team,
Scoring goals like you've never seen."

The producer was listed as Phil Spectator, although it's widely assumed that this was a pseudonym for Jim Simpson. Why the secrecy? Perhaps he didn't want to damage his jazz and blues credibility or, more likely, he didn't want to risk being blacklisted by his beloved Halesowen Town F.C. Whatever the reason, not many records have had the exposure of West Bromwich Albion, regularly heard by 30,000 fans before matches for many years.

Enthused by success, Grandstand Records went on to produce local comedian Dave Ismay's rendition of *A.S.T.O.N V.I.L.L.A* (claret and blue vinyl, of course) and *Meg is Magic*, a heartfelt response to the sacking of much loved star of ATV serial *Crossroads*, Noelle Gordon, aka Meg Richardson.

> Suitably Caribbean, in calypso style, complete with steel drums, West Bromwich Albion was sung by Ray King, ironically a Coventry City supporter

This ATV All Stars line-up includes Jasper Carrott, Jim Smith, Bev Bevan, Robert Plant, Tom Ross and Don McLean

Birmingham City
fans in revolt –
what's that about
history repeating
itself?

WE'RE
BLUE
ARE
YOU?

THE
BOARD
MUST
GO

THE BLUE RE

THE BOAR

The authors – on the outside looking in

About the authors:

Jim Simpson has been prominent on the Birmingham music scene from his beginnings in the 1960s playing trumpet with Locomotive to the present day when he has racked up 37 years as Director of the Birmingham, Sandwell and Westside Jazz Festival and nearly as many guiding the fortunes of King Pleasure and the Biscuit Boys, plus reviving Henry's Blueshouse initially at the Bull's Head, now in the Velvet Music Rooms. When the 1970s dawned, he had recently formed his company, Big Bear Music, now probably the longest lived independent record label in the UK. At the time his main musical involvement was with managing Black Sabbath and running the original Henry's Blueshouse. As the seventies wore on, he toured and recorded many American bluesmen as well as managing and recording such fondly remembered Birmingham groups as Muscles, the Quads and Tea and Symphony. In 2019 Brewin Books published his memoir of 60 years in the music business, *Don't Worry 'bout the Bear*.

Ron Simpson was absent from Birmingham for much of the 1970s, having moved to Yorkshire in 1971. After retiring from teaching in 1995, he has written prolifically. In addition to numerous study guides for English Literature and grammar books aimed at teenagers, he wrote *Teach Yourself English Grammar* which went into its fourth edition in 2019. He also co-wrote *Don't Worry 'bout the Bear*. He reviews theatre and music for several websites and is News and Features Editor for *Jazz Rag*, a national bi-monthly magazine edited by his brother Jim.

The authors would like to thank the following people for their assistance:
Sarah Yang; Mike Olley; John O'Hara; John Parsons; Albert Chapman; Tim Jennings; Charlie Moore; Alexandra Mason; Jasper Carrott; Tony Iommi; Pete Chatfield; Roy Gee Hemmings; Brian Yates; Frank Leadon; Gary Newbon; Chicken George; John Kennedy; Chris Pitt; Andrew Harris; Julia Rose; Deb Wagleigh; Tony Powell; Dave Woodhall; Terry Poole; Terry McGrath; Norman Field; Jim Cronin; Christine Fox; Cheryl Keysell; Barmy Barry; Tom Ward; Alison Clare Farngalo; Debbie Pickering; Malcolm Hill; Bernadette Jarvis; Rose-Marie Smith; April Phillips; Stephen Ward; Alan White; Nigel Smith; Rob Martin; Matthew Edwards; Des Tong; Nick Shaw; Ann Bradley; George Beamish; Ruth Cheshire; Carol Maye; Mark Stephen Reeves; Eileen Vichare; Gillon Jacoby; David Burt; Josep Behan; Wilf Hobart; Sue Fear; Pete King; Chico White; Robin Westley Martin; Kay Medlock; Paul Harris; Maggie O'Connell; Tony Smith; Dave Ward; Paul Weston; David Hadley; Luke James; Norm Elliott; Fran Hawke; Martin Booth; Jonathan Buxton; Martin Hughes; Sheila and Rob Moore; Colette Bayliss; Bethany Green; Arshad Mohammed; Mohammed Arif; Pam Baker; Jonathan Buxton; Gary Evans; Glenn Tranter; Colette Bayliss; Birmingham Past and Present; Birmingham Mail and all members of the Facebook site for Dirty Stop Out's Guide to 1970s Birmingham.